The Dangerous
and the Endangered

The Dangerous Offender Project

JUSTICE

John P. Conrad and Simon Dinitz
Project Co-Directors
The Academy for Contemporary Problems

In Fear of Each Other: Studies of Dangerousness in America   John P.
  Conrad and Simon Dinitz
The Law and the Dangerous Criminal   Linda Sleffel
The Search for Criminal Man   Ysabel Rennie
Out of Circulation: The Dangerous Offender in Prison   Robert Freeman,
  John P. Conrad, Simon Dinitz, and Israel Barak
Restraining the Wicked   Stephan Van Dine, John P. Conrad, and
  Simon Dinitz
The Violent Few   Donna Martin Hamparian, Richard Schuster, Simon
  Dinitz, and John P. Conrad
The Dangerous and the Endangered   John P. Conrad
Justice and Consequences   John P. Conrad
Careers of the Violent: The Dangerous Offender and Criminal Justice
  Stuart J. Miller, Simon Dinitz, and John P. Conrad

**Cover: Cuneiform characters for the word *Justice*, the emblem of the
Dangerous Offender Project.**

The Dangerous
and the Endangered

John P. Conrad

Lexington Books

D.C. Heath and Company/Lexington, Massachusetts/Toronto

Library of Congress Cataloging in Publication Data

Conrad, John Phillips, 1913–

The dangerous and the endangered.

Includes bibliographies and index.
1. Criminal justice, Administration of.   2. Violent
crimes—Prevention.   3. Criminal justice, Administration
of—Ohio—Columbus.   4. Violent crimes—Ohio—Columbus—
Prevention.   I. Title.
HV6025.C593   1985   364   84–28921
ISBN 0–669–02184–9 (alk. paper)

Published simultaneously in Canada
Printed in the United States of America on acid-free paper
International Standard Book Number: 0–669–02184–9
Library of Congress Catalog Card Number: 84–28921

To the memory of Richard and Eleanor McGee whose wisdom and magnanimity still enrich all who knew them

Contents

List of Tables

Acknowledgments

In the beginning was the Academy for Contemporary Problems of Columbus. It began with the excitement of a search for new ways to manage the ordinary business of state and municipal government, including the thankless tasks of crime control and the administration of justice. The Dangerous Offender Project owed a great deal to the support of the academy's president, Ralph Widner, in getting us started, and to his tactful noninterference when we were under way.

Nothing would have been possible without the generosity of the Lilly Endowment, whose trust inspired us to reciprocate with our best efforts. To Richard Ristine, throughout the executive vice-president, and Charles Blair, our program officer, we have tendered our appreciation in our earlier publications, and I do so again with sincerity and friendship.

Many junior colleagues passed through the project and accomplished special tasks. Those who read this book know how much Simon Dinitz and I appreciated their hard work, often of a nature that approached simple drudgery. But that's the kind of work that makes research of this kind possible. Their names will not appear on title pages, nor in these lines, but they all know how much they meant to Simon Dinitz and myself as the project's co-directors.

My gratitude must also go to the senior staff of the project: Ysabel Rennie, Linda Sleffel, Donna Hamparian, Richard Schuster, Stephen Van Dine, and Stuart Miller. Their names are on the title pages of our books. They share in whatever credit this last publication may deserve. Although they have been consulted and their work has been for reference, I will offer them the customary absolution for blame for my own mistakes of commission, omission, or misinterpretation.

Special mention must go to Judy Jacobson, research analyst of the Foundation for Community Planning of Cleveland, Ohio, who generously gave her time to bringing up to date the careers of *The Violent Few* subsequent to the publication of that volume.

The writing of this book was accomplished while I was a visiting fellow of the National Institute of Justice, a distinction conferred on me during the academic year 1982–83 and extended, because of my illness, for 1983–84. My appreciation for the understanding of my Institute colleagues exceeds the usual terms of gratitude. I must particularly mention the support of James Stewart, director of the Institute, Bob Burkhart, John Spevacek, Patrick Langan, and Helen Erskine who dealt efficiently with the obstacles on the way. They could not write the book for me, but it could not have been accomplished without them.

From the earliest days of the Dangerous Offender Project, the collaboration with Lexington Books has been one of the most enjoyable aspects of our work. The professional assistance of Margaret Zusky, our editor, has been indispensable. In an enterprise of this kind, many hands make the work possible, and the expert hands that our publisher has given us deserve more thanks than I can fit into suitable words.

More people than I can name here have given me advice, opinions, and the benefit of their experience. Their names would adorn this page, but I must doubt that their secure reputations would be thereby enhanced.

And finally I must again offer my appreciation to Charlotte Conrad, my wife, who has been patient and interested and who is now glad that it's all over.

The Dangerous and the Endangered

1
Introduction

This book is a consideration of the prevalence and control of violent crime. At a time when publications dealing with this topic abound, justification for yet another is a necessary courtesy to the reader. The world needs no more lamentations or polemics about a condition that neither subsides, as some optimists have predicted, nor plunges the nation into anarchy, as woeful alarmists have so often warned. Remedies are required. Citizens should not be disabled by fears that disorder is the natural state of affairs.

We are accustomed to rely on the criminal justice system to administer the remedies, and I focus here on the relationship between violent criminals and the organs of justice. It is a matter of common sense that most causes of crime are beyond the reach of the state. Legislation and the provision of resources can alleviate poverty, lighten the shameful burden of racism, and assure that inequalities are narrowed by education. In the end, in spite of the commitment of the state to fairness and social justice, some will be poorer than others, prejudice and bigotry will persist, and inequalities will narrow but will nevertheless reflect the unfairness of the human condition. Other changes in our culture are surely more influential. They proceed with inexorable force like the movement of a glacier, beyond the intervention of any human agency: No government can stay the decline of the moral influence of the church, the changes in family and community life, or many other modifications in our national culture.

Nevertheless, the criminal justice system can and should serve us better. For centuries Anglo-American societies have relied on a challenge-and-response sequence to provoke the changes in the administration of justice that are demanded by the nature and volume of crime. If fear of criminals increases, more prisons are built to contain them. If criminals are thought to be sick with criminality, clinicians try to cure them. If the wickedness of some is apparently irreversible, there is a clamor to hang or electrocute them. So it goes, with hypotheses masquerading as principles. Criminal justice has evolved in response to crime on the one hand and, on the other, a revolving succession of dogmas about its causes and control. The dogmas are enthusiastically embraced for a while only to fall eventually out of favor though never entirely discarded.

The novelty of these times is the application of empiricism to the understanding and control of crime. Instead of reacting with speculative notions as to what would be the most appropriate disposition of evil men and women, we collect facts about their behavior, their lives, their response to the laws. An impressive mass of information has been accumulated. We can plan the changes needed in criminal justice in light of facts instead of, or at least supplementing, ancient tradition. It is an only recently possible process, and we still don't know how far it can be carried or what its ultimate outcome will be. We can be sure that along the way there will be many failures and disappointments but now that planning is in earnest, it will continue to be done. It is a necessary support to a legal and administrative structure of rapidly increasing complexity.

I want to contribute to this planning process. My warrant for doing so rests on several years' immersion in the Dangerous Offender Project. With colleagues in Columbus, Ohio, I have been engaged since 1975 in the collection and interpretation of the data of violence in that rather orderly city. It is time to pull together our conclusions and say what they tell the world about violence and the men, women, and children who commit it.

We have completed three empirical studies.[1] For our first report, *The Violent Few*, we collected the records of delinquency of all the youths and children arrested on charges of violence who were born during the years 1956 to 1960. We followed their careers throughout their juvenile years and, in another investigation, continued our observations well into their adult years, with disturbing results (on which I will report in chapter 3).

Our second study traced the careers of men arrested for violent crimes. We drew a random sample of all men charged with homicide, rape, felonious assault, and robbery during the years 1950 to 1976 and traced their criminal histories backward to their beginnings and forward to the time when our study began. The results, with implications that challenge the effectiveness of the present structure of criminal justice, were published in *Careers of the Violent*. They are summarized and reviewed in chapter 4.

For our third study we conducted a statistical experiment to test the potential reduction of violent crime by the incapacitation of the offender. This experiment was reported in detail in *Restraining the*

Wicked, with results that put into perspective the limited relief that can be expected from stringent increases in the restraint of felons. The experiment and its results are summarized in chapter 5.

All these studies were presented in the aseptic vernacular of social science: value-free and data-oriented. We said little about the policy implications of our findings. That style concealed our sentiments. Like other Americans, we were concerned with urban violence—perhaps more concerned than most. Each of us had known men, women, and children who had committed violent crimes and others who had been victims. Each of us had for many years been students of the literature of violence and dangerousness. Intuitions emerging form personal impressions and knowledge convinced us that much could be gained from an empirical study of this phenomenon.

Our studies are complete. Now is the time to say what they tell us about the actions that should be taken. That is my task in this book. It is one thing to tabulate arrest histories and make the indicated cross-tabulations so that interpretations can be dragged out of the charts and tables. It is something else again to prescribe for the control of our population of violent persons. But criminologists should not tie ourselves down to polite exchanges of data communicated in monographs, journal articles, and papers read at annual meetings of learned societies. If our work is worth doing, it must affect the theory and practice of criminal justice. It is good that the mainstream of criminology is now directed toward influencing policy: We are far from the only ones to say what we think should be done.

There is a running symposium on criminal violence in this country, in which all comers freely take part, regardless of their knowledge, experience, or wisdom. Criminologists cannot claim a monopoly of any of these assets, but we must be heard. It is vital that the views exchanged in public discourse should be formed in the light of verified information. The power of a bad idea forcefully expressed can be very great. It is hard to think of any public discourse in which so many bad ideas are afloat, and criminologists have contributed their share. To compete, good ideas must be armed with supporting facts as well as vigorous rhetoric. The data of several years of research are behind me. With the conclusions in hand, I now plunge into the national symposium on violence, well aware that my views are at variance with those of many of my peers, as well as with the encrusted assumptions that pass for conventional wisdom.

The Problem

Violence infects our cities at a time when more and more Americans are living in them. In less-fortunate countries, urban disorders are "revolutionary" campaigns of anarchic disruption based on ideologies exploiting the genuine miseries of the dispossessed. In U.S. cities, violence consists of the random acts of the predatory and desperate. The consequences to our society are no less grave than the purposeful terror inflicted by political dissidents. An organized cell of armed insurrectionists can be defeated by planned and resolute action. Street criminals must be caught and restrained, one by one.

Fear of crime has become durably endemic. Sometimes it is an irrational fear, unrelated to the facts of city life. Violence in our major cities has led citizens in less-afflicted communities to suppose that equivalent dangers await them on their more peaceful streets. Their fear is real, even though the risk is not. The sense of danger is not easily allayed by the traditional administration of justice. It spreads through the culture, creating new myths and reviving old bigotries. We are in danger of becoming a nation of paranoids.

The peace of the city has always been precarious. Accounts of city life in centuries past such as the *Autobiography of Benvenuto Cellini* and the *Diary of Samuel Pepys* vividly describe the dangers in Renaissance Florence and the violence in Restoration London. In this country, social historians have only begun to assess the extent of crime in eighteenth- and nineteenth-century Boston, New York, and Chicago. Crime in nineteenth-century Columbus, the site of these studies, and then a peaceful town of less than 40,000 population, has been recalled by Eric Monkkonen.[2] As might be expected, the low crime rates he found contrast with the turbulence of the metropolitan centers on the Atlantic seaboard.

Tracing the data as far back as they can, some criminologists have concluded that the rates of violent crime have been relatively stable for generations. Most cities, they think, have always contained dangers for ordinary people. By this perception of our social history, the mounting fear of violent crime in the late years of the twentieth century does not correspond with any increase in danger.

Whether these conclusions are historically justifiable or statistically tenable (and I doubt it) is irrelevant to the policy riddle that confronts all branches and all levels of government in this country. The public may be mistaken in its belief that violent crime is out of control and that the institutions that are intended to suppress it are unable to do so. Those who hold such a belief will not be comforted by criminologists who parade historical data to the contrary.

It hardly matters if violent crime rates are no worse than they always have been: What does matter is that more must be done to bring them down. It is a confession of impotence to defend the present state of affairs with assertions that crime has always been a serious and insoluble problem and citizens must therefore learn to put up with it. Contemporary Americans have learned to expect more of government and, as to the violence on the streets, seek a sense of urgency from that government.

Many useful measures have been taken, and they cannot be ignored. The police are better trained and better equipped than ever before. Every element of criminal justice has been subjected to research and evaluation. The system has begun to experiment, and that is a gain over the speculative assumptions frozen into dogma that used to underlie policy and law. We know far more than ever before about how many crimes are committed, how often, by whom, and to whom. Despite the smug conclusions of less-than-competent program evaluators, we even know that some measures of intervention and control work very well with some offenders. We also know that some criminal men and women do not respond to any interventions short of outright and prolonged incarceration. We even have a fair idea of how such offenders may be identified.

These accomplishments show that much can be done first by thinking carefully about what needs to be done and then by experimenting with measures for doing it. Eventually criminal justice will be administered within a frame of tested principles rather than time-honored notions. To paraphrase Socrates, an unexamined theory is not worth retaining.

But offsetting the progress of the last twenty years is the dismal record of unabated crime. It is natural to suppose that improvements in the criminal justice system should bring about results that can be measured in greatly lowered crime rates. So far nothing of the sort has happened. The public is not to be convinced that its expectations of criminal justice are excessive or unrealistic. It feels that the combination of an efficient new technology and appropriate severity in the administration of the police and the courts should clear the streets. If the efficient use of technology is not enough to make the streets safe, then the hard line should be harder. Demands are heard for laws that would restore and extend the use of the death penalty. Mandatory prison terms for the major crimes have been enacted, and their lengths have been doubled and sometimes more than doubled. Improvident initiatives are rushed into legislation to reassure the angry and fearful public that the system is responding.

The severity that is soaking into the criminal law has not diminished the dread. The streets still *seem* dangerous, whether they are or not. Many citizens firmly believe that violent men, women, and children roam the cities, unrestrained and flouting all efforts to restrain them.

The crime problem lends itself to the proposal of simple solutions. No matter how often the solutions fail, they are so plausible in principle that they can always be peddled again. Public officials and legislators spend time, energy, and their public credit in ardent advocacy of ineffective nostrums such as the restoration of capital punishment, the imposition of mandatory life sentences, and the legislative removal of juvenile court jurisdiction over children charged with crimes of violence.

All these measures sound tough and look cheap, which accounts for their smooth passage through the legislative mills. Their effect on the just administration of the laws must be judged by accumulating experience, but the economic costs are already great. Immense sums of money are committed to maintaining and operating our prisons, and more must be spent on building new cages. Not many citizens give much thought to what they are getting for their money. Those who do get the reputation of cranks who are soft-hearted and unthinking allies of the nation's criminals. It is typical of the administration of justice in the United States that little consideration is given by governors, legislators, or even by some penologists to the uses to which prisons, jails, and youth "training schools" are put. Once they are built, they contain criminals, and that is enough. For a while these unworthy Americans are off the streets and out of the way of more solid citizens.

Irrationality does not always prevail. Seminars, workshops, and institutes in criminal justice have as their objective the deliberate improvement of the administration of the laws. The longer that a problem is considered, the more likely that its previously unappreciated difficulties will loom in their true magnitude. More research is called for, task forces are mobilized, and pilot experimental projects are designed. The vocabulary may be pretentious, and it is easy to deride the theorizing in ivory towers, far above the precinct stations, the squad cars, and the holding tanks. I have participated in these blackboard adventures myself but nevertheless must insist that most innovative changes in criminal justice have started on blackboards, though preferably in collaboration with working professionals. Changes are always less than sweeping, and benefits are less than prodigious, but the cumulative improvements have removed criminal justice from the grubby, low-grade politics and opportunism that have characterized its administration throughout our history.

Rational new responses to crime will not sweep the thugs from the streets. Incapacitation will reduce their number, but not by as large a percentage as some enthusiasts hope. The recruitment of new criminals will probably be deterred—a little—by the severe penalties enacted by tough legislators, but citizens should not suppose that criminals are as responsive to deterrence as common sense and enlightened self-interest would dictate. Irrational men and women, when inclined to thuggery, will listen to reason only when in their muddled minds it seems to their short-range advantage to do so.

Rationality is the indispensable ingredient of any system. It is the main defense of a civilized society against the anarchy to which unrestrained criminality must lead. The control of crime requires the full attention of the whole society—not just the criminal justice system.

My objective is limited. There must be and there can be a better defense against criminal violence. The elimination of crime is an unattainable goal, and so is the Utopia in which social justice always prevails. The principal role of criminal justice is to administer the consequences of the criminal act to the criminal who commits it. Those consequences must be sufficient to denounce the crime and to bring the criminal into firm control. When this is well and fairly done, the system has done all it can. My task is to propose ways to improve the effectiveness and the fairness of the system.

The Underbrush

The central figure on this stage is the *dangerous offender.* Implicit in that term is intellectual underbrush that must be cleared away before we can give the offender our undivided attention. Some of this underbrush is semantic, so tenuously semantic that readers may compare me to a medieval scholastic as I address myself to defining terms. Careless use of language has obstructed clarity of thought about dangerousness, and clarity is essential if we are to achieve its solution. I begin with the vocabulary of dangerousness. (Bear with me and my definitions; I shall not be long at this task.)

The fundamental source of muddle is the use of the words *violence* and *danger.* For some writers and more speakers these words are synonymous. Here I shall strive for rigor. For my purposes, violence is the character of an act in which bodily harm is inflicted or threatened. Some writers extend the term to all sorts of undesirable activities. Some say that the sale of narcotics is a violent act. Some will so characterize the pollution of the environment, the oppression of the poor, or the greed of the rich. I have heard famous politicians described as the "most violent men in America," men whose conduct has been far from admirable but who have prudently avoided even the appearance of violence, let alone the commission of overt acts.

In this consideration, I shall refrain from metaphors where I can and certainly will avoid the contamination of these fundamental words with rhetorical usage. I need *violence* as a term to characterize specific categories of crime: homicide, forcible rape, aggravated assault, robbery, and arson. These are the crimes of violence that are tabulated as such by the Federal Bureau of Investigation in the annual *Uniform Crime Reports*. They generate the anxiety on the streets and the chaotic condition of the criminal justice system today.

In the suggestive definition of Sarbin,[3] *danger* denotes a relationship. It is a relationship between the dangerous person and other persons whom he may harm or to whom he may threaten or attempt harm. It may be a relationship between the dangerous person and some specific other person—as when the betrayed husband sets out to kill the man who cuckolded him. It may be a relationship between the dangerous person and many but random others—as when the pistol-carrying hoodlum goes out to make a few scores mugging unwary citizens on dark and lonely streets. The desire for revenge for a real betrayal may underlie danger to a specific betrayer, but to no one else. More to my point is the danger presented by armed young men seeking to enrich themselves by intimidation.

To say that a person is dangerous is to *predict* that he or she will at some future time commit a violent crime, that the criminal justice system may be helpless to prevent. If the dangerous person is not committably insane, he cannot lawfully be restrained until he has committed a crime. Even if he has committed an offense, he must be charged, tried, and sentenced for that offense and not for his inclination to be violent. Can this limit on the social control of violent men be loosened? Some of my colleagues believe that methods can be developed that will place such criminals under the control that public safety requires without unfairness to the innocent or the nonviolent.

For many years, criminologists have devoted much attention to methods of predicting future criminal behavior. Their success has been modest at best, and as to the prediction of violence nothing has been offered that judges are willing to accept. I shall return to this problem in chapter 6. Here I call the reader's attention to a formidable obstacle to the use of *danger* as an acceptable term for use in the administration of justice. If the ascription of *dangerousness* to an offender rests on a prediction of his future conduct, and if such predictions cannot be made reliably, the idea of the dangerous offender must be reconsidered. There may be a way out of this quandary, and in chapter 7 I shall offer my solution.

A criminal's past is thought to be the best predictor of his future. A man who has committed many violent offenses in the past may be expected to continue in his violent ways. Since the early years of this century, legislators have seized on this truism to empower the courts to sentence offenders as *habitual criminals*, using many kinds of offenses to establish the existence of a habit.[4] Most judges have made little or no use of this power. In both the United States and in England, people who commit grave violent offenses are almost always eligible for long terms in prison without imposing the special status of habitual criminality. We shall see that there is indeed such a person as an habitual criminal. So far, most jurisdictions, with a few remarkable exceptions, have been able to deal with him without the encumbrance of a special label.

That takes care of the immediately necessary definitions; there will be more as the later chapters are unfolded. There are other matters, however, on which understandings must be sought before we can go on to substantive matters.

The Limits of Empiricism

Although criminal statistics are kept in much better shape than ever before, there are still gaps in our knowledge, and some of the gaps are not open to empirical closure. Expedients have been proposed for other gaps. Many criminologists are committed to the opinion that self-reporting questionnaires and interviews can provide valid data on uncleared crimes. Reliance on data of this kind for the further development of policy, as urged by some writers,[5] seems a dubious course to more traditionally oriented policy-makers.

Uncertainties about the true rate of certain crimes, especially the violent offenses, persist because of the almost universal practice of "negotiated" justice. In many jurisdictions (though not at present in Columbus), an armed robbery can be pled down to a lesser offense, and so can an aggravated assault.

Despite these and other persisting obstacles to statistical purity, improvements in counting and reporting crimes and convictions probably will continue in the years to come. Americans have been kind to statisticians and have learned to rely heavily on their findings in fields as diverse as the money supply and the earned-run averages of major league pitchers.

What will long defy consensus is the interpretation of data for the creation of new policy. Ideological commitments and ordinary differences of opinion will lead to widely divergent propositions derived from the same sets of figures.

For example, in many states a rapid growth of prison population has followed a comparable increase in the crime rates. To those committed to a policy of severity in the treatment of criminals, that was to be expected. If there are more criminals caught committing more crimes, there should be more convicts sent to prison. The inevitability of this relationship could be expressed as a mathematical pair of variables: Incarceration rates are functions of crime rates.

An opposing view holds that these data demonstrate the futility of incarceration. It neither deters potential criminals nor does it reform or intimidate those who are subjected to penal servitude. It follows that these data merely express the national waste of money on useless prisons that produce nothing but misery and alienation, and thereby confirm criminals in their antisocial ways.

Each side in this passionate debate claims common sense and the data as allies. More data will not settle the difference. The essential information is in the hands of both disputants. The empiricist can set the boundaries for reasoned argument, but, as in most human affairs, agreement on the essential facts cannot control decisions that depend on attitudes.

This contribution to criminal justice discourse presents my own interpretation of the body of knowledge that my colleagues and I have amplified with the findings of the Dangerous Offender Project. That enterprise forced me to change some of my views concerning future policy developments. Whether others will be led to change their views remains to be seen. I hope that at least the unshaken and the unconvinced will be induced by our findings to reformulate arguments that have gone stale.

Notes

1. Donna Martin Hamparian, Richard Schuster, Simon Dinitz, and John P. Conrad, *The Violent Few* (Lexington, Mass.: Lexington Books, 1977); Stephan Van Dine, John P. Conrad, and Simon Dinitz, *Restraining the Wicked* (Lexington, Mass.: Lexington Books, 1979); Stuart J. Miller, Simon Dinitz, and John P. Conrad, *Careers of the Violent* (Lexington, Mass.: Lexington Books, 1982).

2. Eric H. Monkkonen, *The Dangerous Class: Crime and Poverty in Columbus, Ohio, 1860–1885* (Cambridge, Mass.: Harvard University Press, 1975).

3. Theodore Sarbin, "The Dangerous Individual: An Outcome of Social Identity Transformations," *British Journal of Criminology* 7(1967):258.

4. Linda Sleffel, *The Law and the Dangerous Offender* (Lexington, Mass.: Lexington Books, 1977).

5. See Jan M. and Marcia R. Chaiken, *Varieties of Criminal Behavior* (Santa Monica: Rand Corporation, August 1982). See also Peter W. Greenwood with Alan Abrahamse, *Selective Incapacitation* (Santa Monica: Rand Corporation, August 1982).

2
The Law and Dangerousness

Prevention by Example

As early as Plato[1] philosophers have urged that the objective of the criminal law should be the prevention of crime, but statesmen and lawyers have until recently been almost exclusively preoccupied with the punishment of criminals. Cesare Beccaria[2] and Jeremy Bentham[3] are generally credited with the reintroduction of crime prevention as a significant theme in criminal law. A review of the legal history does not uncover much evidence that crime prevention was a serious goal for which the criminal justice system could be held responsible until late in the nineteenth century. Our police, prosecutors, judges, and prison wardens were busy catching criminals and punishing them and gave little thought to reconstruction of the law for purposes of crime prevention. If the punishment of criminals could not protect citizens from predation, protection would have to be sought from sources other than the administration of justice.

The rigors of punishment, as practiced for millennia, were imposed with the expectation that terror would intimidate the "dangerous classes" composed of the supposedly envious and desperate poor. The cadavers of highwaymen swung from cross-roads gibbets in Tudor England,[4] and hideous executions were inflicted on criminals such as the unfortunate Damiens, who attempted to assassinate Louis XV;[5] these must have been intended to convey a message as well as to retaliate upon the bodies of the criminals. The use of the law for general deterrence always has had firm advocates. The sentiments of Sir James Fitzjames Stephen, that quintessential Victorian "hard-liner," express a point of view that was not new in his time and that some hold today:

> I would punish with death offences against property only with great deliberation, and when it was made to appear by a public formal inquiry held after a conviction for an isolated offence that the criminal was an habitual, hardened, practically irreclaimable offender. . . . I suspect that a small number of executions of

professional receivers of stolen goods, habitual cheats, and ingen-
uous forgers, after a full exposure of their career and its extent and
consequences, would do more to check crime than twenty times
as many sentences of penal servitude. If society could make up its
mind to the destruction of really bad offenders, they might in a very
few years, be made as rare as wolves, and that probably at the
expense of a smaller sacrifice of life than is caused by many a single
shipwreck or colliery explosion.[6]

This is the utilitarian position, starkly put by a judge who prided
himself on his virile realism and was certain that strenuous measures
had to be taken if crime was to be prevented. The infliction of the
death penalty for crimes less heinous than murder or treason will
not find many open advocates today, but the spirit of severity that
seemed imperative to Stephen is once again prevalent.

To hang a particularly notable fence—as Stephen thought might
be proper—is said to prevent crime by example. One by one, criminals are punished with sufficient severity so that like-minded peers
will take heed before they embark on similar careers leading to similar ends. For a utilitarian this is the application of a sound principle,
however extreme past practice may have been. The principle continues to be in vogue, but English and U.S. legislators are groping
toward definitions and procedures that will identify whole classes
of offenders for deterrence and incapacitation on the presumption of
dangerousness. With many uneasy reservations about the feasibility
of such a project and its ethical implications, "positivist" criminologists have begun to collect and interpret data that might make
possible more effective control of men, women, and children with
propensities for violence. The prospects for success are bleak. During
this century the application of this plausible idea in the courtrooms
of several countries has dismally failed to match the expectations
of jurists and theorists.

The positivist idea is rooted in early criminology. The doctrines
of Cesare Lombroso, the founder of criminal anthropology, are safely
stowed in the memory hole of social science, but his taxonomy of
offenders survives despite the crudeness of his terminology: We still
speak of "born criminals,"[7] "insane criminals," and, most significant
for this project, "habitual criminals."

The notion that persistence in crime should be given special
attention in legislation and by the courts seems to have been first
articulated by the German criminologist, Franz von Liszt in 1882.[8]
Segregation from society was the obvious answer to such persistence,
von Liszt held, arguing from a firmly positivist stance that the law

should focus on the criminal rather than the crime. It was a contagious idea, but extraordinarily difficult to translate into an acceptable statute. In most European countries some kind of habitual offender legislation was enacted in the years before World War II.[9] The passage of statutes presented moral and semantic problems that plague conscientious legislators to this day.

Preventive Detention in England

The English experience demonstrates the perplexities that confront legislators, prosecutors, and judges in that country and wherever the segregation of persistent criminals is seen as a desirable goal for criminal justice. In 1895 Herbert Gladstone, as chairman of a committee on the state of the prisons reporting to the House of Commons, put the solution in these words:

> When an offender has been convicted a fourth time or more he or she is pretty sure to have taken to crime as a profession and sooner or later to return to prison. We are therefore of opinion that further corrective measures are desirable for these persons. . . . We venture to offer the opinion that that a new form of sentence should be placed at the disposal of the judges by which offenders might be segregated for long periods of detention, during which they would not be treated with the severity of first-class labour or penal servitude, but would be forced to work under less onerous conditions. As loss of liberty would to them prove the chief deterrent, so by their being removed from the opportunity of doing wrong, the community would gain.[10]

But how long should a "long period of detention" be? From what crimes would the community be protected? In the first draft of the statute, the length of the term of segregation was left up to the Prison Commissioners. In the judgement of influential members of Parliament, that was too much discretion for an administrative office to be allowed. After years of debate of this and other issues, the Prevention of Crime Act was passed in 1908 with a maximum term of fourteen years.

Criticism of this law was persistent, vigorous, and without significant effect until 1948, when a new Criminal Justice Act was approved. The 1908 law had provided that a convicted offender could be sentenced to preventive detention after three felony convictions *and* if it were shown in court that he had been "leading persistently a dishonest or criminal life." That phrase proved to be "troublesome," to use the word of the Director of Public Prosecutions, who pointed out that interludes of honest employment in an otherwise fully committed criminal career were frequently cited as evidence of the intention to lead a law-abiding life.

In spite of this and other difficulties, 1,095 offenders were sentenced to preventive detention between 1909 and 1948. Their average age ranged from 38 in 1910 to 55.7 in 1939. A review of the 325 cases sentenced between 1928 and 1945 found that the last offenses of which they were convicted were overwhelmingly nonviolent property offenses. There were two robberies, three "woundings," and one arson, and one "extortion by threat."[11] If the act was intended to protect the public from violence, it was not supported by evidence of violence in the statistics accumulated over this long period. Indeed, of these 325 terminal crimes, 66 were "simple and minor larcenies."

This was not the kind of protection that the Gladstone Committee intended. In a Home Office memorandum presented to Parliament in 1911, the purpose of the Prevention of Crime Act was clarified, to no apparent effect:

> Only the great need of society to be secured from professional or dangerous criminals can justify the prolongation of the ordinary sentences of penal servitude by the addition of . . . preventive detention. . . . [T]he bill was devised for the "advanced dangerous criminal," for the "most hardened criminals": its object was "to give the State effective control over dangerous offenders": it was not to be applied to persons who were "a nuisance rather than a danger to society," or to the much larger class of those who were partly vagrants, partly criminals, and who were to a large extent mentally deficient."[12]

In spite of this unambiguous restatement of the original intent of the act, persistent offenders were sentenced under its terms, and dangerous offenders were not. In their review of the history of legislation for habitual offenders, Floud and Young account for this apparent misapplication of the law:

> First, . . . petty thefts or frauds might inflict more serious injury on victims of slender means than major thefts or burglaries committed against persons of wealth. Second, serious offences in themselves justified long sentences of imprisonment as punishment within the normal range, so the question of protection did not arise.[13]

The Criminal Justice Act of 1948 set out to correct this anomaly. The criteria for a sentence to preventive detention called for the prisoner to be,

1. not less than thirty years of age,
2. convicted of a felony punishable with imprisonment of two years or more,
3. thrice previously so convicted since attaining the age of 17,
4. sentenced, at least twice previously, to borstal training or imprisonment,
   and
5. the court must be satisfied that preventive detention is expedient for the protection of the public.[14]

Confirmed recidivists could be sentenced to terms ranging between five and fourteen years, but detention was to be differentiated from the rigors of the ordinary prison. Younger recidivists, those between age 21 and 30, were to be dealt with more leniently in a regime of "corrective training" of between two and four years in the belief that there was still hope for them if they were immersed in a program of remedial education, vocational training, and hard work.

Neither regime was satisfactory in practice. In 1967 Parliament tried again, producing this time the concept of an "extended sentence," under which the courts could lengthen the sentence imposed up to a maximum of ten years. And again, the practice focused almost entirely on persistence in property crimes rather than the demonstration of repetitive violence. "If ever there was a case of a distinction without a difference, the substitution of 'extended sentence' for 'preventive detention,' must be it, in spite of a change in the legal definitions used," wrote Barbara Wootton, a staunch advocate of common sense in the administration of justice.[15] According to Floud and Young, it was applied in 129 cases in 1970, and use declined to 4 in 1976. "Of the 75 extended sentences imposed between 1974 and 1976, only 12 (16%) were in respect of crimes against the person."[16]

There the law stands—in a state of pronounced desuetude. Floud and Young, writing for the Working Party on Dangerous Offenders, proposed new legislation that would address itself solely to the future violence of offenders rather than to their past persistence in crimes against property, sometimes rather petty crimes. Their proposals would lead to legislation providing for the following safeguards against the repetitively violent offender:

PRINCIPAL PROPOSALS OF THE WORKING PARTY
ON DANGEROUS OFFENDERS[17]

1. The sentencing of "dangerous" offenders should be the subject of legislation. It is desirable that the distinction implicit in the present sentencing practice of the courts, between the ordinary and the exceptional "dangerous" offender, should be formalised so as to facilitate a substantial reduction in the length of sentences for imprisonment for ordinary offenders (not excluding those whose offences are the worst of their kind) whilst continuing to provide a necessary measure of protection for the public against the exceptional, high risk, serious ("dangerous") offender.

2. The wholly indeterminate life-sentence of imprisonment should cease to be available for non-homicidal offences and the use of determinate sentences of imprisonment for the protection of the public should be statutorily controlled.

3. No protective sentence of imprisonment (i.e. no sentence of imprisonment which, in order to protect the public against a risk of future harm, is made longer than would be justified on other grounds alone) should be imposed on an offender unless the following conditions, to be provided by law, are satisfied.

4. The law should provide that:

(i) The public should be entitled to the protection of a special sentence only against grave harm: *grave harm* should be interpreted in this context as comprising the following categories: death, serious bodily injury, serious sexual assaults, severe or prolonged pain or mental stress, loss of or damage to property which causes severe personal hardship, damage to the environment which has a severely adverse effect on public health or safety, serious damage to the security of the State.

(ii) Subject to the restrictions in (iii)–(vi) and the safeguards in (vii)–(ix) below, the Crown Court should be empowered, for the protection of others against grave harm by an offender, to sentence him to imprisonment for a specified period greater than that which would ordinarily be specified, but proportional to the gravity of the anticipated harm and the court's estimate of the duration of the risk: such a sentence should be called a protective sentence;

(iii) a protective sentence should not be imposed unless the court is satisfied that by reason of the nature of his offence and his character, conduct, and antecedents the offender is more likely to do further grave harm than other grave offenders of similar age and sex and that there is no other permissible way of dealing with him which offers the necessary degree of protection for the public;

(iv) an offender should be eligible for a protective sentence only if he has done, attempted, risked, threatened or conspired to do *grave harm* as defined in (i) above *and* has committed an act of a similar kind on a separate occasion from the instant offence;

(v) a protective sentence should not be imposable for murder or manslaughter so long as the life sentence is available for these offences: but the life sentence should not be available for any other offence;

(vi) a protective sentence should not be imposed on an offender who is below the age of 17 at the time of sentence, nor on one who is eligible, by reason of his mental condition, for a hospital order under the Mental Health Act 1959, unless, though eligible, he cannot be placed in a suitable hospital;

(vii) a protective sentence should not be imposed without giving the offender prior indication that the judge has this in mind, so that he may prepare his arguments against such a sentence;

(viii) before imposing a protective sentence on the offender the court should receive full reports from the following: a psychiatrist, on his mental condition, with particular reference to the possibility that he may be eligible for a hospital order under the Mental Health Act 1959, the police, on the nature and circumstances of his offence and record of past behavior, and a probation officer, on his background and circumstances. These reports should be prepared in the knowledge that the court is considering a protective sentence;

(ix) should the court decide that a protective sentence is necessary for the protection of the public, it should state its reasons for so deciding;

(x) the cases of offenders so sentenced should be reviewed by the Court of Appeal (Criminal Division): they should be referred to the Court at once, without the procedure of making an initial appeal to the single judge for leave to appeal, with the effect that his application can be heard direct by the full court before whom he will be legally represented;

(xi) a protective sentence should entail the minimum curtailment of the offender's liberty compatible with its purpose: such a sentence will be initially served in custody but the offender should be released on licence at the earliest opportunity. The conditions of licence should favour specific rather than general curtailments of liberty;

(xii) the decision to release an offender on licence and to modify or terminate the conditions of the licence should rest with the Home Secretary for the duration of the sentence imposed by the court, subject to his receiving the recommendations of an independent Review Tribunal of quasi-judicial composition and character to which the prisoner should have right of access, and the further advice of an Advisory Board charged to consider his suitability for release or changed conditions of licence, with special reference to the public interest in his continued detention;

(xiii) a prisoner released from custody in the course of a protective sentence should be subject to licence involving supervision by the probation and after-care service and the possibility of recall to prison until the sentence imposed by the Court has expired. On the recommendation of the Advisory Board the Home Secretary should be empowered to require an offender to obey the conditions of a licence of a further period, not exceeding three years, after the sentence imposed by the Court has expired, if he is of the opinion that this is desirable in the public interest;

(xiv) The Review Tribunal should consider the case of an offender as soon as practicable after a protective sentence has been passed and should fix the date for first review: in no case should this be later than that on which the prisoner will have served one-third (or whatever fraction (at present one-third) as would determine his eligiblity for parole from a non-protective sentence) of the sentence imposed by the court or three years, whichever shall be less. The Tribunal should thereafter review his case at intervals of not more than two years.

This is a cautious proposal, calculated to assure that no offender subject to it will be locked up and the key thrown away and that the dangerous offender will be treated with discriminating firmness. It also includes offenses that, though reprehensible enough, are certainly not violent in the literal sense understood by the ordinary citizen. Nevertheless, it would be impossible for a judge to impose a protective sentence on a petty thief or even on an "intolerable nuisance."

The report of the Working Party has been published. Reviewers have approved, the quality of the hard work has been recognized, and nothing has happened in Parliament. A transatlantic observer must suppose that the dynamics of change in the administration of justice in Great Britain resemble those in the United States. The only proposals likely to capture enough attention to initiate action and pursue it to a statutory conclusion are those designed to correct flagrantly dangerous conditions. The Working Party's thoughtful recommendations will be a resource stored until events demonstrate the existence of such conditions.

The Habitual Criminal in the United States

Legislation intended to control of dangerous offenders had a much later start in the United States than in England, but its success in achieving objectives has been just as meager. In 1926 the New York legislature passed the Baumes Act, under which anyone convicted of a third felony may be sentenced to a minimum of fifteen to twenty-five years and a maximum of life—the latter requiring a finding by the court that the character of the defendant and the nature and circumstances of his criminal conduct indicate that prolonged incarceration and lifetime supervision will best serve the public interest.[18] Forty-two jurisdictions followed with habitual offender statutes of their own. Only eight states have resisted the trend: Illinois, Maryland, Massachusetts, Mississippi, Ohio, Pennsylvania, Utah, and Virginia.

Although most of this legislation is intended to incapacitate the violent offender who is considered dangerous, these statutes are so loosely drawn that in many jurisdictions any recidivist, whether violent or not, may be eligible for a commitment to prison as an habitual criminal. In only six states is eligibility for habitual offender status limited to offenders guilty of violent instant crimes; in contrast, thirteen states permit commitment of persons who may have been guilty of misdemeanors only.

The range of permissible sentences is wide: from mandatory life terms to a schedule of augmentations depending on the offender's recidivist status. The Connecticut law is typical of many such statutes:

Status at Instant Offense	*Allowed Penalty*
Second misdemeanor theft	Up to 3 years
Third 3rd or 4th degree larceny	Up to 5 years
Second felony	Up to twice maximum for instant offense
Second violent offense[a]	Life, if court finds it in the public interest

[a]Limited to manslaughter, arson, rape, kidnapping, first- or second-degree robbery, first-degree assault.[19]

It is hard to generalize about the usefulness of statutes of this kind in controlling dangerous offenders. In recent years, severity in sentencing has been greatly enhanced in a number of states that obviously intend to restrain persons considered dangerous or, perhaps, intolerable nuisances. As matters stood in 1977, however, Sleffel was surely justified in her conclusion that

> [H]habitual criminal laws, since they do not even by their own terms attempt to distinguish violent from nonviolent offenders, and since they are subject to so much discretion, must be considered of little use in singling out and dealing with violent offenders.[20]

Sleffel's dismissal of habitual criminal legislation was not accompanied by empirical data on the frequency of its use or other analysis of its effectiveness—it would have been difficult indeed to design a project to collect such data and interpret them—but her conclusion was hardly an isolated comment. The very infrequency of the use of these statutes and the probability that their principal value was in plea-bargaining support her view.

For at least twenty years, legal scholars have tried to improve on the clearly ineffectual legislation described in this chapter. In 1962 the American Law Institute published the Model Penal Code, which contained a carefully drafted section on the extension of sentences for certain kinds of offenders who presented special dangers to the public. This code provided that an extended term of imprisonment could be imposed on a person convicted of a felony if the court found that he was

(1) a persistent offender whose commitment for an extended term is necessary for the protection of the public.

(2) a professional criminal whose commitment for an extended term is necessary for the protection of the public.

(3) a dangerous, mentally abnormal person whose commitment for an extended term is necessary for the protection of the public. Such a finding required a psychiatric examination resulting in a conclusion the defendant's mental condition is "gravely abnormal," that his criminal conduct is characterized by compulsive behavior or by persistent aggressive behavior, and that "such condition makes him a serious danger to others."

(4) The defendant is a multiple offender whose criminality was so extensive that a sentence of imprisonment for an extended term is warranted.[21]

In 1968 the American Bar Association published a proposal for new sentencing standards that provided for discretion for the trial court in determining whether a sentence was to be extended and by how much. The rules set forth in these standards provided that

(i) any increased term which can be imposed because of prior criminality should be related in severity to the sentence otherwise provided for the new offense;
(ii) the sentencing court should be authorized to fix a maximum term at any point from the maximum otherwise applicable up to a legislatively prescribed limit. As an outside limit for extreme cases, twenty-five years ought to be the maximum term;
(iii) the court should be authorized to fix a minimum term in accordance with the principles stated in section 3.2, i.e., a period of time, "reasonably short," to be served before an offender becomes eligible for parole, and to be imposed only after a finding that such a term is necessary to protect the public from further criminal conduct by the defendant.

Further, the standards prescribed that extended sentences should be imposed only for a third felony conviction, if less than five years have elapsed between the instant offense and the last previous conviction, and if the offender was more than age 21 at the time of the commission of the new offenses.[22]

Commenting on the provisions of these standards, the drafting committee noted that

The penal laws of this country reflect practically universal agreement that persistent offenders should be subject to greater sanctions than those who have been convicted for the first time. . . . [T]his consensus has led to an indefensibly harsh sentencing structure which has produced a series of brutal results. . . . [I]t is often a characteristic of these statutes that they require the imposition of a life sentence after the conviction of four, and not so rarely, three felonies. Not so common are statutes like the one in Nevada, which requires a life sentence for the sixth conviction of petty larceny. In Washington, five convictions for petty larceny require the imposition of a life sentence, while three must be followed by a term of ten years.[23]

The committee commented further that where habitual offender laws are mandatory in terms, the discretion will reside with the prosecutor. As an example of the consequences of discretion exercised at this level, a 1956 study of West Virginia application of a particularly severe law (adding five years to the maximum sentence for any second felony) was cited, showing that of 904 defendants eligible for prosecution as recidivists, only 79 were actually so prosecuted. The committee concluded that

> it is unsound for habitual offender statutes to provide a mandatory prison term which must be imposed regardless of the circumstances of the offense. . . . As the sentence increases in severity, the possibilities of injustice increase, as do the possibilities of uneven enforcement due to widespread nullification.[24]

The movement in jurisprudence to create model legislation has flagged. Several states adopted variants of the Model Penal Code, among them, Hawaii, New Hampshire, North Dakota, and Oregon. But the interest of legislators, bench, and bar was diverted in the 1970s to the perception that something had to be done about the nation's indeterminate sentencing laws: The creation and study of models lapsed into undeserved oblivion.

The Mandatory Determinate Sentence

The habitual offender laws, whether or not enlightened by either the Model Penal Code or the Model Sentencing Act, were not repealed. Some states use them a great deal: In Texas, for example, about 10-percent of the prison population is serving life terms under the provisions of the habitual offender laws of that state. In most states, movement was toward increasing the penalties for crimes most abhorred by the public. Assurance that severity would not be abridged by future parole board leniency was gained by adopting determinate sentence structures for the major crimes of violence and, in some states, for all felonies.

The criterion for a "protective" sentence in the United States is not mere persistence in crime or a judgment that an offender or class of offenders may be dangerous to the public. These kinds of decisions are open to differences of opinion, but at least opinion may be informed by simple data: A defendant has been sentenced for major felonies on a specified number of previous occasions, or an offender's criminal record contains clear evidence of associations with an organized gang prone to violent acts. Included increasingly in the criteria is heinousness: An offender's crime is so outrageous that he will be sent down the road to prison for years and years, perhaps the rest of his life, perhaps without possibility of parole. Aside from the rapid accretion of long-term prisoners beyond the capacity of prisons to accommodate them, subjective criteria must lead inevitably to injustices fermented by prejudice, facilitated by incompetent defense, or coerced by intimidating prosecutors who use a terrifying law to obtain an easy plea-bargain. There can be little question that the public now accepts almost any degree of severity in dealing with the street crime. Nevertheless, the certain consequences of violence in the prisons, the high cost of justice, and the probable incidence of injustice require that the excesses of our mandatory penalties be corrected.

Notes

1. The most famous quotation is to be found in *Protagoras* at 321: "punishment is not inflicted by a rational man for the sake of the crime that he has committed . . . but for the sake of the future, to prevent either the same man or, by the spectacle of his punishment, someone else, from doing wrong again. . . . [A]t all events the punishment is inflicted as a deterrent." Accounts of the administration of justice in ancient Greece and Rome do not indicate that Plato's precept was a guide to practice.

2. Cesare Beccaria, *On Crimes and Punishments*, translated by Henry Paolucci (Indianapolis: Bobbs-Merrill, 1963), 93–99. In the noble language of this last chapter, Beccaria claims that egalitarian citizenship is the sovereign preventive of crime, but this author was a practical man, well aware that eighteenth-century Europe might acclaim its humanity but find its application too arduous. Observance of the laws came first: "It is better to prevent crimes than to punish them. This is the ultimate end of every good legislation. . . . Do you want to prevent crimes? See to it that the laws are clear and simple and that the entire force of a nation is united in their defense. . . . See to it that men fear the laws and fear nothing else. For fear of the laws is salutary."

3. Jeremy Bentham, *Works*, vol. 1 (Bowring edition, New York: Russell, 1962), 396. "General prevention ought to be the chief end of punishment, as it is its real justification. . . . [A]n unpunished crime leaves the path of crime open, not only to the same delinquent but to all those who may have the same motives and opportunities."

4. Georg Rusche and Otto Kirchheimer, *Punishment and Social Structure* (New York: Columbia University Press, 1939), 19. According to this source, about 75,000 men were hanged during the reign of Henry VIII alone. The authors do not state their authority for this statistic, commenting that the data must be "approximately correct."

5. Michel Foucault, *Discipline and Punish*, translated by Alan Sheridan (New York: Pantheon Books, 1978), 3–6.

6. James Fitzjames Stephen, *A History of the Criminal Law of England*, vol. 1, 1883 (New York: Burt Franklin, n.d.) 479.

7. The term *born criminal* no longer finds its way into circumspect scientific discourse, but the idea that criminal behávior has genetic antecedents does not die easily, as witness the recent flurry about the XYY chromosomal anomaly or, more subtle, the theories of Samuel Yochelson and Stanton Samenow. See their *The Criminal Personality* (New York: Jason Aronson, 1976).

8. Details of the history of this idea can be found—by those who are sufficiently interested—in untranslated German treatises by von Liszt. A rather murky account of Liszt's contribution and the late nineteenth-century discourse concerning it can be found in Marc Ancel, *Social Defence, A Modern Approach to Criminal Problems*, translated by J. Wilson (London: Routledge and Kegan Paul, 1965), 48–50.

9. Any student of the early history of habitual offender legislation must acknowledge a debt to Norval Morris's *The Habitual Criminal* (London: Longmans Green, 1951). Regrettably, no comparable history of the development of habitual offender law has been made since the publication of Morris's exhaustive history.

10. *Report of the Committee on Prisons*, 1895, *op.* 31 (quoted by Morris, *The Habitual Criminal*, 34).

11. Morris, *The Habitual Criminal*, 62–65.

12. Quoted in Jean Floud and Warren Young, *Dangerousness and Criminal Justice* (London: Heinemann Educational Books, 1981), 79.

13. *Ibid.*, 79.

14. Morris, *The Habitual Criminal*, 251.

15. Barbara Wootton, *Crime and Penal Policy: Reflections on Fifty Years' Experience* (London: George Allen and Unwin, 1978), 105. Lady Wootton's position is rigorous (p. 246):

> [T]he protection of the public is the only unchallengeable justification for locking anybody up. . . . [T]he period of detention should be governed only by the likelihood that a prisoner would be a danger (or perhaps one should add, an intolerable nuisance) to others if he was released. . . . If imprisonment is necessary only to keep the dangerous out of harm's way, it would appear that many sentences now imposed in the middle range (say, from 18 months to 5 years) are unnecessarily long, while in other cases an alternative to imprisonment or a suspended sentence might have been preferable. We have no evidence that that longer sentences in this range carry a lesser risk of recidivism than shorter ones.

This position, combining as it does economy and humane policy, is a clear call for penal innovation, to which neither English nor U.S. penologists have adequately responded. If faithfully adopted, it would surely ease the overcrowding problem and in many jurisdictions the results would be fiscally very significant.

16. Floud and Young, *Dangerousness and Criminal Justice*, 81.

17. *Ibid.*, 154–57.

18. Linda Sleffel, *The Law and the Dangerous Criminal* (Lexington, Mass.: Lexington Books, 1977), 1.

19. *Ibid.*, 6.

20. *Ibid.*, 19.

21. *Ibid.*, 33, reproducing section 7.03 of the *Model Penal Code* (American Law Institute, 1962).

22. American Bar Association Project on Standards for Criminal Justice, *Standards Relating to Sentencing Alternatives and Procedures* sec. 3.3, *Habitual offenders* (New York: Institute of Judicial Administration, 1968), 160–62.

23. *Ibid.*, 162.

24. *Ibid.*, 166–67.

3
Violence and the Juvenile Offender

Solicitude and the Hard Line

Americans have shifted from a tradition of indulgence to children in trouble to an angry fear of violent juvenile offenders. A demand for the restraint of supposedly dangerous children has replaced the solicitude that called for their rehabilitation under the auspices of the juvenile court.[1] The change is recent and momentous. It is too early to estimate its effects on the rates of crime and delinquency, on the youths committed to prolonged custody, or on the deterrence of potential delinquents in the community. The evolving "hard line" draws on the daily news and on imperfectly interpreted statistics. Dread and anger, not a resolution to solve a problem, have determined the changes in public attitudes and the speed with which they have been transformed. A fearful nation has been led to believe that a new strain of violence has infected U.S. youth. Legislatures and the judiciary respond to that perception without investigation of its authenticity. The administration of juvenile justice must respond to the realities of crime and delinquency, but our understanding of urban violence is surely insufficient to justify the harsh new legislation that has been proposed and, in some states, enacted into law.

With these considerations guiding us, our plan for the Dangerous Offender Project began with a study of violent juveniles in Columbus. That part of our project was reported in *The Violent Few* in more detail than anyone not engaged in criminological research could possibly want to read.[2] Those who wish more than the supporting data that I intend to furnish here are invited to refer to our full account. In this chapter I shall restrict myself to a summary and the minimum number of tables necessary to follow my argument and understand our principal findings.

From Philadelphia to Columbus

Our method owed much to the classic study by Wolfgang, Figlio, and Sellin of delinquency in a birth cohort in Philadelphia.[3] In that research, a cohort was formed comprising all the boys born in Philadelphia in the year 1945 who lived in that city between their tenth and eighteenth birthdays. The object was to discover how many of these boys became delinquent, how many delinquent acts of what kinds they had committed, and how often they had committed them. The findings now stand as a benchmark known to every criminologist and, I suppose, to most professionals in the administration of justice. For convenience, because we adopted some of their methodology and made comparisons of our findings with theirs when we could, I shall recapitulate here the conclusions most relevant to our Columbus study.

There were 9,945 boys in the Philadelphia cohort. Their careers were traced through their records in schools, police stations, and courtrooms until the end of their juvenile years. A sample of the cohort was followed well into adulthood.[4] Of this large group, 3,475 (34.9 percent) were delinquent at least once. Within that total, 627 (6.3 percent of the whole cohort, 18.0 percent of the delinquents) were *chronic offenders*, a term that was reserved for those who had been arrested five or more times. These chronic offenders were responsible for 51.9 percent of all the delinquencies committed by the cohort. That amounted to 5,305 offenses, of which 1,008 were crimes against the person.

That finding is famous. It confirmed the intuitive judgement of police officials that a small number of men and boys commit most of the crime in large cities. It is contended that if these people could be swept off the streets for a suitably long time, those streets would be much safer. The merits of this recommendation are certainly debatable, but it has inspired some innovative proposals for the incapacitation of various categories of offenders. I shall return to this topic in later chapters.

A less celebrated finding was also important for our research. The Philadelphia group was interested in the desistance of juveniles from further delinquencies. Their data enabled them to investigate the probability that any offender would proceed from a first to a second offense, from a second to a third, and so on: The calculations were pursued to the fifteenth transition.[5] They found that the proportion of boys desisting after the first offense was much greater than after any subsequent offense. After the second offense the probability varied that still another would be committed, but less significantly for all further transitions.[6] Later in this chapter, it will be seen that the study of these transitions assumed great importance for our analysis of the "velocity" and duration of delinquent careers.

The Questions for the Columbus Cohort

We narrowed our universe to juvenile violent offenders, about whose careers we wanted to learn more than our Philadelphia colleagues had told us. To qualify for our study, an offender had to have been booked by the police on at least one charge of violence. We created a cohort comprising all the boys and girls[7] born during the years 1956 to 1960 who had been arrested at least once by the Columbus police for a violent offense and who had lived in Franklin County—which encompasses Columbus and its numerous suburbs—during the course of a delinquent career. That produced 1,222 individuals.[8] What could they tell us about juvenile violence?

Our search for answers began with two specific questions:

1. What are the social and criminal characteristics of juvenile offenders arrested for violent offenses?
2. What relationship do these characteristics bear to identifiable delinquent career patterns?

Certainly the youths in our cohort were unusual. In 1970, when they ranged in age from 10 to 14, they constituted 1.44 percent of the population in this bracket in Franklin County. The boys were 2.5 percent of all the boys in this age group. The known violent juveniles in Columbus were about two out of every hundred—hence our title, *The Violent Few.*

There were 1,469 arrests of our cohort members for offenses with elements of violence, ranging from physical resistance to arrest to the index crimes of violence—homicide, assault, rape, and robbery. They were certainly not all the violent offenses perpetrated by Franklin County youths, nor were they all the violent offenses committed by members of our cohort. Many crimes are never cleared by the police. Our youths must have committed some of them. Self-reported delinquent histories compiled in other studies suggest that some offenders commit a surprising number of crimes before they are caught. It is reasonable to suppose that there are at least a few who are never caught.[9] Finally, there must have been some transient juveniles who committed a mugging or an assault while residing temporarily in Columbus and were never apprehended. With all these reservations conceded, we still had a cohort of youths prone to some violence but small compared to the population of their nondelinquent peers.

We expected that the data collected in this research might help in settling the validity of five prevailing notions about juvenile violent offenders and planned our first data sweeps accordingly. The notions we wanted to test were these:

1. *The intensive delinquency of the chronic offender.* The Philadelphia research had shown that chronic offenders committed a greatly disproportionate number of serious crimes. We wanted to know whether our recidivists had committed a comparably disproportionate number of offenses, how serious those offenses were, and the extent to which these youths specialized in violence. If there was a substantial number of such specialists, legislative and policy changes might be indicated.

2. *The long career of the early delinquent.* A postulate of criminology since the early work of Sheldon and Eleanor Glueck,[10] holds that the earlier the onset delinquency the longer will be the youth's criminal career. Although we could not project the careers of our delinquents into their adult years within the time limit for publication of *The Violent Few*, we retained our files for later analysis when our youths had passed into adulthood. My report in this chapter relies on an analysis of the delinquent careers of our cohort members continued up to age 23 to 28. It includes many whose careers were limited to one arrest—in some cases, long ago—and many others who have not yet ended their depredations. From these data we expected to determine the degree to which the Gluecks' generalization is true for the most feared juvenile offenders as far as we could track them.

3. *The linear progress from bad to worse.* It is frequently asserted that juvenile offenders begin with trivial violations of the law such as the "status offenses" (infractions of the law applying only to juveniles, such as truancy, curfew violations, and "incorrigibility"), and then go on to much more serious offenses. This prediction looks like plain common sense to some observers. Like so much common sense when tested in the data of crime and delinquency (which do not record acts conceived in the cool light of reason), it might not survive empirical scrutiny.

4. *The young monster.* Pessimists seize gloomily on the idea that the disintegration of parental, church, and school authority has brought into being a mutant generation of vicious and sadistic young people who commit horrifying crimes for their depraved

enjoyment. This view is especially common among citizens who combine overexposure to a little social science with a shuddering anticipation of social doom. While we knew of some boys who might qualify as "monstrous," we didn't know of many, and hoped that a study of our cohort might shed light on their relative frequency.

5. *The extinction of violent careers.* Criminologists believe that as offenders grow older they "mature" out their criminal careers. Whether maturity in the usual sense of that word has anything to do with the ending of a career of juvenile delinquency seemed doubtful to us, but it is important to know how many violent youths ended their delinquency while still young, even if we could hardly expect to find out why or what became of them later.

All these notions deserved our attention. None seemed likely to be proved wholly wrong. All tended to oversimplify a complex mixture of causes and effects. Juvenile justice cannot respond to all the complexities in the real world, but it must discriminate among real young people in ominously serious trouble—for themselves and everyone around them. We intended that our study would contribute to more precision in juvenile justice policy-making, where sweeping generalizations have so often settled most issues for legislators, judges, and public, and, so often tragically, for the children whose fates are thus decided so early in their lives.

The Findings

Once the questions are asked, the pick-and-shovel work of social research begins. We worked within limits we did not set. We could not collect original data for this cohort, prepared by our own standards of proof. We relied on persons who had no responsibility for meeting the requirements of research in preparing their documents. They could not know that their work would find its way into our hands for purposes unrelated to its intended use. The police officer writing a booking, the social worker collecting face-sheet information for the juvenile court, and the receiving unit personnel of the Ohio Youth Commission all had administrative objectives when they made their contributions to the records of our violent few. We were looking over their shoulders, making their data serve double duty. Their questions were intended to inform decision-makers of the facts needed to make appropriate decisions, or to enable managers to classify and program the offenders assigned to them. We would have had to ask most of these questions for our purposes, but there were others that we would have wished to ask but were not on the administrative agenda.

A computer can sort the data into categories and then quantify the categories, but it can capture only the realities that can be expressed in numbers. For this study we could never investigate the "under-the-roof" cultures found in the homes of our delinquents that was important to the Gluecks[11] and was important to us, too, but inaccessible with our methodology. Nor could we make any headway with the various subcultures represented in our cohort. No instruments we could have designed, no method we could have contrived for this research could elicit from the information we had borrowed any findings more subtle than the comparative effects of the crudest influences on our delinquents.

More could have been done with unlimited time and money. In Utopia we might have enlisted the unreserved assistance of busy officials and the confidence of offenders and their families. But we were working in Ohio, not Utopia, and our resources were not bottomless. Our work was a contribution to an understanding of the problem, perhaps leading to an eventual improvement of its current resolution. It could not answer all the questions about juvenile violence that we might have asked, nor could it lead to all the definitive conclusions that juvenile justice practitioners need. With that warning, I now proceed to an account of our principal conclusions.

The Human Material

There was a heavy overrepresentation of blacks, males, and the poor in our cohort of 1,222 youths. In the 1970 census the population of Franklin County was 12.5 percent black, but there were 662 blacks in our cohort, or 54.2 percent of the total. The overrepresentation of boys was even more pronounced (always the case in studies of this kind): 84.5 percent of the cohort was male, 15.5 percent female.

To get a rough idea of the economic circumstances of the families of our youths, we resorted to the expedient of locating each delinquent's residence in its census tract. Each tract could be classified according to the median income of its population. The distribution of income that results is necessarily crude, but it will be seen that nearly half of our cohort lived in poor or very poor parts of town. Our sociodemographic variables are displayed in table 3–1.

Table 3–1
Distribution of Cohort by Sociodemographic Variables[a]

	Number	*Percentage*
Race		
Black	662	54.2
White	560	45.8
Total	1,222	100.0
Sex		
Male	1,033	84.5
Female	189	15.5
Total	1,222	100.0

Distribution of Cohort Subset, 1956–1960 By Socioeconomic Status.[b]

SES		
Very poor	74	6.5
Poor	512	45.0
Moderate	389	34.2
Above median	163	14.3
Total	1,138	100.0

[a]Data provided by Federation for Community Planning, Cleveland, Ohio.
[b]Source: Hamparian et al., *Youth in Adult Courts: Between Two Worlds* (Columbus, Ohio: Academy for Contemporary Problems, 1982), table 3–3, p. 44. This distribution not available from Foundation for Community Planning.

The Violence They Committed

A completed delinquent career ends at age 18 in Ohio; after that the adult career of crime begins. As juveniles they were arrested for a total of 4,481 times on 55 different charges, ranging from 20 homicides to 363 curfew violations. Table 3–2 shows the distributions of the 1,469 arrests for violent offenses.

We found that 374 of our cohort of 1,222 (30.6 percent) were arrested only once, necessarily on a charge of violence. (It should be kept in mind throughout this chapter that many of the arrests were for offenses that were minimally violent.) For the rest, the number of arrests ranged up to 23, the latter a record achieved by only one youth. The average number of offenses for the whole cohort was 4.0, but for the 848 youths who committed more than one offense, the average was 5.2. Over four-fifths of the cohort (84.6 percent) were arrested for only one violent offense. There were only 24 (2.0 percent) who were arrested for two or more violent crimes but had no other arrests.

Our delinquents were no specialists in violence or any other variety of offense. According to Klein, there has been a common

Table 3–2
Distribution of All Arrests on Charges of Violence
(total cohort, N = 1,222; total arrests = 4841)

Charge	Number	Percentage
Homicide	20	0.4
Rape	72	1.5
Robbery (unarmed)	191	4.0
Armed robbery	39	0.8
Aggravated robbery	139	2.9
Purse snatch	178	3.7
Assault with intention to rob	28	0.6
Assault	549	11.3
Aggravated assault	119	2.5
Sexual imposition/sodomy	40	0.8
Molesting	91	1.9
Intentional stabbing	2	0.04
Negligent homicide	1	0.02
Subtotal	1469	30.4
All other charges	3372	69.6

Source: Data provided by Federation for Community Planning, Cleveland, Ohio.

assumption that "many or most juveniles show specialization in offense types and a progression over time from less to more serious categories of offenses. These assumptions are particularly well fixed in the minds of practitioners who use them as part of the rationale for behavior-specific treatment modalities and early intervention strategies." Klein reviewed thirty-three studies of delinquent careers completed between 1963 and 1982 (including *The Violent Few*) and found that thirty of these investigations arrived at the conclusion that delinquent careers follow a "cafeteria-style" pattern, to adopt his less-than-felicitous metaphor.[12]

Klein remarks that he is "uncomfortable" about the consensus of research that he has discovered.[13] The implication is that there should be patterns, and perhaps there are, but that no one has found firm evidence that patterns of delinquent behavior exist that can be detected in arrest records or self-reported histories. I suggest as an hypothesis for eventual investigation that once a juvenile has engaged two or more times in delinquency he or she is released from some, most, or all of his scruples. This condition must be particularly true of a boy or girl who has engaged in serious violence. A burglary, a till-tapping, or an auto theft will seem readily acceptable to a youth who has passed the threshold of serious crime. Wherever an opportunity appears his only restraint will be his estimate of the risk of apprehension. Any criminal opportunity that presents itself to a boy or girl past this threshold may be accepted, especially if friendly peers are there to join him.

The Dangerousness of the Chronic Offender

There were 378 chronic offenders (30.9 percent) in the whole cohort of 1,222. That compares with 18.0 percent of the delinquent set in the Philadelphia study, which included a substantial number of non-violent delinquents. Each member of our cohort had committed at least one act of violence, but except for the one-time offenders, only 24 had limited themselves to violent crimes. Our chronic offenders were disproportionately delinquent. Nearly two-thirds (64.8 percent) of all the arrests for the whole cohort were for offenses charged against these recidivists. There were 105 youths (8.6 percent) who were arrested ten or more times. They accounted for more than a quarter of all the cohort's arrests.

Most of our chronic offenders had engaged in a wide variety of offenses. Some were nothing more than simple assaults, sometimes a schoolyard fist fight for which the police were summoned. Without making a post hoc subjective judgement on each arrest report, there was no satisfactory way of winnowing out the relatively minor crimes of violence from those that were grave felonies by any measure.

Many offenses were serious. The cohort was responsible for 397 aggravaged offenses, of which 158 chronic offenders (12.9 percent of the entire cohort) committed 221 (55.7 percent). Note that there were 220 chronic offenders whose offenses did not qualify as "aggravated," though there were a substantial number of unarmed muggings, an offense that most citizens would not wish to dismiss as a minor escapade. By no means every chronic offender, even in this cohort of violent juveniles, was a serious threat to the community, but this end of the cohort was responsible for more than four times its share of the most serious delinquencies.

Eighty-one youths (6.6 percent) achieved chronic status before age 14. Undoubtedly each was maladjusted to the prevailing norms and a potential burden to the community. We traced their careers as closely as we could, but so far as we could discover they were not disproportionately destructive. They committed 9.5 percent of the cohort's aggravated crimes against the person. Their early start on their delinquent careers did not threaten the community so much as it damaged themselves. Hardly any—if any at all—had ended their series of delinquencies before age 18. In one way or another, as prisoners or jailbirds, as welfare dependents or derelicts, they and their like will probably be public charges for many years to come. Keeping in mind that a substantial fraction of our cohort was composed of boys and girls who were no more than nominally violent, table 3–3 is reproduced from *The Violent Few* with some diffidence.

In this table we arbitrarily defined homicide, forcible rape, aggravated robbery, and aggravated assaults as aggravated violent offenses. We added in all other arrests for violent crimes except those for misdemeanor assaults and sexual molestation. The statutes regarded these two latter categories as less serious, and we accepted this boundary, a decision that is certainly debatable. However, from the data presented here, it seems that about one-third of our chronics were no great threat to the community. They were troublesome individuals and their prospects as they aged into adult years indicated more trouble to come.

The Long Career of the Early Delinquent

In the entire cohort, there were 392 who were delinquent before age 13—including two who somehow were arrested at age 6. Of this set of early delinquents, 150 were still being arrested at age 17, including one of those two six-year-old early starters. So far, there does not seem to be an inevitably long career in crime ahead of the early delinquent. As we shall see later in this chapter, as time went on and youths became men and women, some of the careers of crime that seemed to be interrupted were resumed.

Table 3–3
Distribution of 378 Chronic Offenders by Number of Violent Offenses Committed

Number of Violent Offenses	Number of Chronic Offenders	Percentage
None[a]	133	35.2
1	173	45.8
2	58	15.3
3	8	2.1
4	5	1.3
5	1	0.3
Total	378	100.0

Source: Data provided by Federation for Community Planning, Cleveland, Ohio.

[a]The offenders counted here were misdemeanants charged with battery or sexual imposition.

The policy implications of this analysis are uncertain. As will be made clear later on, no consistent juvenile court policy determined the disposition of these juveniles. Less than half found their way into state and county incarcerative facilities, and custodial control seemed to speed up rather than retard the resumption of delinquencies. Most of our cohort were subjected to nothing more severe than a judicial rebuke and a term of nominal probation.

Early delinquency need not be regarded with unrelieved pessimism. Pre-adolescent children who are delinquent should be the first priority of those who must make decisions about their disposition. With careful planning they can be steered into harmless futures. With decisions made by rule of thumb, or worse, with a good plan but slovenly execution, the early delinquent becomes a heavy public charge.

The Linear Progress from Bad to Worse

I hope that our research can bring into question a persisting item of conventional wisdom—the notion that "status offenders" are beginners in serious criminal careers. Our data challenge that supposition. No more than 10 percent of our cohort began with a referral to the juvenile court for a status offense. That is an inconspicuous fraction of our cohort, most of whom qualified as the most serious juvenile offenders in Columbus. However, I must acknowledge that there is a dark figure for status offenses. No data were available to test the thoroughness of school attendance enforcement, the effectiveness of curfews, or the willingness of parents of our youths to file pleas of incorrigibility in the juvenile court. Nevertheless, it probably does not stretch credibility to suggest that the percentage of "unrulies" in our cohort did not exceed the unruliness of the general population by much more than indicated by the percentage given here. Probably an even larger fraction of the general population is guilty of one of these violations, though not haled into court.

In 1974 the Franklin County juvenile court heard 599 charges of "unruly behavior" (Ohio's umbrella term for the status offenses). The "unrulies" in our cohort were an insignificant fraction of that total. Whatever the future holds for the status offender, a career of violence is improbable. Unruly youths are problems to themselves and to everyone around them. Their prospects in an industrial or postindustrial society are dim indeed. But only a few of them are headed for lives of crime and incarceration. There must be other means for their control than the administration of juvenile justice.

As for the truly delinquent boys and girls, our data provided only murky answers to the question of progression from bad to worse or better. To get a perspective on the kinds of progression to be found in our cohort, we divided each delinquent career, no matter how short or how long, into thirds. With this trichotomy we located each violent crime in the sector of the career in which it occurred. This stratagem produced a simple table, which I reproduce here (see table 3–4).

If any tendency at all is to be discerned here, it is for the violent offense to occur early in the career rather than as a culmination. The differences to be seen among the locations of the first arrest for violence are not great, and no one should suppose that a rule can be derived from this finding. It can be said, however, that although there are some delinquents who go from bad to worse, there are others who seem to go from bad to better—at least for a while.

Our attention was drawn to the youths who were arrested only once. In the complete cohort of 1,222 there were 374 such individuals. Of that number, 166 (44.4 percent) were arrested on charges of index violence—homicide, forcible rape, aggravated assault, and robbery. But inspection of arrest reports indicated to us that many of these youths were caught in situations that were difficult to excuse but that did not augur a future in crime—as the lack of further arrests suggested in the cases of the younger "singletons." On the other hand, a single arrest at age 16 or 17 might be the first in a prolonged adult criminal career. Inspection of adult records uncovered 135 youths who were arrested as adults. There was no way that we could inquire further into the characteristics of the singletons who desisted for good.

In short, the many single arrests contradict the notion that there is a linear progress that delinquents must follow once started on a downward slope, even though many first arrests are only the beginning of extended criminal careers. Distinctions are to be made, and

Table 3–4
Distribution by Position of First Arrest for Violence
(1956–58 Subset, N = 811; in percentages)

		Three or More Arrests			
Single Arrests	Only Two Arrests	First Career Third	Second Career Third	Third Career Third	Total
29.5	23.1	23.1	17.6	13.7	100.0

Source: Hamparian et al., *Youth in Adult Courts*, 67. These data were not revised by the Federation for Community Planning.

these distinctions cannot be based solely on statistical probabilities. They must rest on responsible judgments of factors that cannot be captured in mathematical calculations. In the administration of juvenile justice, someone must know a great deal about the boy or girl before the court before any decision is made.

The Young Monster

The sponsor of our project was inspired—if that is the appropriate word—by the exploits of an oversized and precocious fourteen-year-old boy who terrorized and humiliated some residents of a middle-class Indianapolis neighborhood. Armed with a shotgun and accompanied by two older but apparently subordinate companions, he robbed and publicly raped the patrons of three retail establishments. To assure a safe departure from the scene of their crimes, the perpetrators forced their victims to disrobe. When he was finally apprehended, the press luridly referred to him as a "monster boy." It was natural to speculate on the origins of his behavior. Psychologists could readily discover a lot of psychopathology in his early childhood, about which it was too late to do anything.[14] It was also natural to speculate on the number of boys like him who might be roaming the streets, the danger they presented to innocent citizens unrecognized by anyone. We looked for young monsters in our cohort, so far as we could with the data on hand.

In our cohort of 1,222, there were 42 young men who had committed two or more aggravated violent offenses in which serious physical harm was inflicted or threatened. If monsters were to be found in our cohort, the first place to look for them would be among these 42 boys. We traced their careers as far as we could, which was not beyond age 28 for the oldest in the group.[15]

This small subset contained some exceptionally violent youths. As juveniles, they were arrested on a total of 302 occasions. The median number of these arrests was 6.0. Within this total there were 84 arrests for violent offenses. That included 4 murders, 8 arrests for forcible rape and 8 for "gross sexual imposition," 28 aggravated robberies, 7 unarmed robberies, 13 aggravated assaults, 10 simple assaults, and 6 arrests for "other violence." Six of the 42 had been bound over to an adult criminal court, where 3 were convicted of murder, 2 of armed robbery, and 1 of forcible rape.

As adults, they compiled a mixed record. Nine have not been arrested for anything, and 12 more have limited themselves to arrests for nonviolent offenses. The remaining 21 have been arrested for index violent offenses on a total of 33 occasions. As of the end of

1983, 17 were serving time in prison—6 on their second term, 3 on their third, and all before age 28.

We could investigate no further. Certainly not all of these 42 young men were qualified monsters, and perhaps that designation could not be applied to each of the six who were sent to prison as adults while still technically juveniles. Some may have been dangerous youths like the boy whose depredations in Indianapolis "inspired" our project. We know far too little about the inner turmoil that projects such youths into repeated and outrageous delinquencies. They and their like deserve another study of a far different kind than ours—a study that would focus on the traits that propelled them into their destructive conduct. In the case of the Indianapolis "monster boy," reviews of his school, police, and court records uncovered plenty of signs that much was seriously wrong. Hindsight told the story of missed opportunities to divert him from the swath of violence that almost surely will make him a lifelong outlaw. Foresight might not have been effective, but, as nothing was tried, nothing will be known. Young monsters are rare birds requiring individual study rather than the statistical computation of their frequency.

The Extinction of Violent Careers

In our cohort of 1,222, there were 721 who went on to active careers as adult offenders. They were arrested for a total of 2,958 times after age 18. Few, if any, had clearly desisted from criminal behavior by the end of the follow-up study in August 1983. Table 3–5 displays the distribution of the entire cohort, showing the numbers of subjects beginning their delinquent careers before each age from 13 to 17 and presenting the numbers and percentages of beginners who ended their careers before each age indicated.

It would be encouraging to observe that 41 percent of our subjects were arrested for the last time before reaching age 18 if we were sure that all of them were out of trouble for good. That was not the case. Some were incarcerated, some must have been between offenses— or arrests—some may have left Ohio, some may have died, and, perhaps, some have not been caught lately. We did find that 125 members of the subset were under the control or supervision of the Ohio Youth Commission on their eighteenth birthday. They could be expected to resume their delinquent careers as soon as they were free to take advantage of attractive opportunities, as some of them did.

Still, the steady rise in cumulative percentages of those who had

Table 3–5
Number of Subjects in Cohort by Age of First and Last Arrest
(N = 1,222)

Age of First Arrest	Age of Last Arrest													Total	
	12		13		14		15		16		17				
	N	%	N	%	N	%	N	%	N	%	N	%		N	%
12 or younger	69	17.6	9	2.3	34	8.7	47	12.0	83	21.2	150	38.3		392	100.1
13			61	30.1	14	6.9	21	10.3	33	16.3	74	36.4		203	100.0
14					81	34.3	27	11.5	51	21.6	77	32.6		236	100.0
15							70	44.9	23	14.7	63	40.4		156	100.0
16									74	62.2	43	36.8		117	100.0
17											118	100.0		118	100.0
Total	69	5.65	70	5.73	129	10.56	165	13.50	264	21.60	525	42.96		1,222	100.00

Source: Data provided by Federation for Community Planning, Cleveland, Ohio.

been arrested for the last time suggests that a substantial number of violent delinquents terminate their careers before they reach adult years. We don't know enough about the extinction of deviant behavior to suggest the policy implications.

The question is vitally important. Incarceration is seldom beneficial to those incarcerated, and such benefits as it may confer diminish in value as it is protracted. It is also expensive, especially with juvenile offenders, for whom an educational regime is ordinarily prescribed in addition to the increasingly costly routines of security. Its use should be limited to need. When an individual's criminal propensities are close to extinction—if we could discern such a phase in an uncertain process—the measures of control should decline in rigor. Not nearly enough is known to make rules for safe decisions in the disposition of youths who have qualified as violent offenders. Pending enquiries that will increase the guidance available to judges and probation officers for assessing the extinction process, those who make policies and decisions should bear in mind the varied trajectories of youthful delinquent careers. However alarming the delinquent acts of adolescents may be, there is a real chance that their careers will not be long. Responsible judgment in individual situations may improve on the unpromising statistics.

Mining the Data

The simple questions posed and answered so far were by no means all that our data could tell us. We now had a fair idea of the dimensions and composition of our cohort and its subsets. We could lay out some of the trends and test some of the notions about serious delinquency that have been entertained by professionals in juvenile justice. What else could we learn from this mass of information that we had dredged up from the files of the juvenile justice system of Franklin County? Some of our most important findings emerged from a further statistical analysis of our tabulations. I shall summarize.

Race

The black component of our cohort was more than half the total, or three times the black share of the Columbus population. That finding was not unexpected. Most studies of urban delinquency arrive at a comparable overrepresentation. Going on to examine dispositions and outcomes, we found that there were no major percentage differences in the distributions of white and black offenders. *Once a boy or girl has become seriously delinquent, that status is more important in determining the immediate future than race or any other characteristic.*[16]

Blacks tended to commit robbery, both armed and "strong-armed," more often than white youths. Whites were arrested a little more often for rape and assault. None of these differences was significant enough to conclude anything about race as a determinant of any particular kind of delinquency.

Delinquency is a personal disaster that befalls too many black children. The causes are documented in the literature of race relations. There is no need to recite the painfully obvious black grievances in a society that begrudges so many the right to an equal start and later a fair stake. Remedies are slow to take effect, even in a prosperous and generous city like Columbus. While their parents await economic and social parity, too many black children hustle their way into trouble. Criminologists have a way of rediscovering what everyone has known all along, and we were no exceptions. Our finding is uncomfortable for the comfortable classes, but it must be kept in sight along with similar findings going back over many decades. Racial injustice is no reason to condone criminal acts, but until it is healed the statistics for urban violence will continue to bloat.

The Prediction of Dangerousness

Human behavior does not lend itself to the prediction of future events—of either the offenses of youth or the decisions of judges. Our next question demonstrated the truth of this proposition. We wanted to measure the consistency of the Franklin County juvenile court in disposing of complaints against members of our cohort. We reasoned that if the judges and referees were predictable in their decision-making, it would be generally known among the youth of the county with, possibly, some deterrent effect. We could test the consistency of decisions by determining how well we could predict the actual decisions by constructing a predictive system from the available social and criminological variables. In a series of exercises made possible by the computer, we found that no combination of criminal histories and demographic data, no matter how they were selected and weighted, could account for the variance of the decisions above a level of 50 percent. That meant that there was no consistency with any of the statistical variables usually employed to predict criminal behavior.

At the top of the scale, no actuarial system is needed to predict that youthful murderers and rapists will be locked up. The courts were consistent at that level; when the verdict was guilty there was no alternative to extended confinement. The significance of this finding may not be as immediately apparent as its importance warrants. The tradition of the juvenile court calls for decisions to be made in the child's best interest. To make such a decision, the court must begin with an estimate of the child's future as it might be affected by the several possible choices. The range extends from dismissal to indeterminate incarceration. In practice, though, when a boy or girl has committed a murder, the feasibility of any alternative to incarceration vanishes. The juvenile guilty of the gravest crimes must be restrained. All other choices become moot.

A lot of children were incarcerated on nonviolent charges, as shown on table 3–6. Inspection of the arrest histories suggested the reason. Judges tried to avoid committing first offenders to the Ohio Youth Commission, even if the offense were rather serious. Later such an offender might be brought before the court again for a less serious offense or for one of a sequence of minor offenses. Eventually judicial patience would be exhausted. The result in a statistical table would be an anomaly. Some offenders would be packed off to a state facility for minor offenses, while others with more serious instant violations but still at an early stage in a delinquent career would be tried on probation. The Franklin County Juvenile Court was often disappointed, but its optimism survived.

When a judge is confronted with a boy or girl in trouble for the first time, his decision to give the kid a break is not only understandable but often correct. So is a decision to accept that child's promise to straighten out if given just one more chance. As we have seen, nearly a third of our cohort were arrested only once and were never heard from again. About 16 percent of the second offenders did indeed "straighten out" (see table 3–4). The result of this kind of individualization is a policy dilemma. To aggregate hundreds of lenient decisions and scores of apparently harsh decisions produces a system from which undesirable inferences will be drawn: The system is unpredictable, a gamble for a daring boy or girl. Almost all of them know that they cannot get away with murder, but they have good reason to know that short of murder, or some crime close to murder in seriousness, the chances are good that they won't have to do time. The chances are better than fair that if a boy or girl is not sent off to a training school, the alternative sanction will not be stringent.

Is this the way the system should work? Opinions differ widely. Many critics argue that a policy of the least possible intervention

Table 3–6

Distribution of Dispositions by Number and Percentage for Juvenile Offenses

(N = 1,222. 4,841 charges)

Dispositions	Aggravated Violence	Other Violence	Property	Public Order	Drugs	Misdemeanor	Assault and Battery	Total
				Offense Groups				
Institutional commitments								
Number	275	38	303	40	31	68	41	796
Percentage	33.2	24.4	19.4	8.6	18.6	6.7	6.4	16.4
Jail or detention								
Number	77	34	205	57	22	172	101	668
Percentage	9.3	21.8	13.1	12.3	13.2	16.8	15.8	13.8
Formal supervision								
Number	107	30	292	66	30	101	119	745
Percentage	12.9	19.2	18.7	14.2	18.0	9.9	18.6	15.4
Informal supervision								
Number	118	25	419	205	38	497	211	1513
Percentage	14.2	16.0	26.8	44.1	22.7	48.7	33.0	31.25
Incomplete (disposition pending, unknown or "other")								
Number	62	11	107	30	6	129	36	381
Percentage	7.5	7.1	6.8	6.4	3.6	12.6	5.6	7.9
Dismissed (includes "complaint withdrawn," and not guilty)								
Number	190	18	237	67	40	54	132	738
Percentage	22.9	11.5	15.2	14.4	23.9	5.3	20.6	15.2
Totals								
Number	829	156	1,563	465	167	1,021	640	4841
Percentage	100.0	100.0	100.0	100.0	100.0	100.0	100.0	

Source: Federation for Community Planning, Cleveland, Ohio.

will best serve the interests of both the child and the community. This view is dismissed by the "hard-line" advocates who urge increased severity to intimidate the individual and to deter his peers. We do not think that our data will settle this debate and doubt that any data could. Whatever is to be done to change the system should not be based on statistical prediction. Certain prediction is impossible by any method. We concluded that if the system could never predict with certainty the behavior of a youth in trouble, the youth should be able to predict what the system will do to him if he commits an offense. That does *not* mean that we advocated the increased commitment of minors to any kind of incarceration. There are other and better solutions, to which I will return in chapter 7.

The Velocity of Recidivism

One common-sense assumption about the imposition of sanctions
on offenders, adult or juvenile, holds that the more severe the punishment the more effective the deterrence of the delinquent so punished. It follows in the reasonable common sense of ordinary citizens
that when a boy receives a mere reprimand from the bench for his
serious offense he will be more likely to resume his delinquencies
than if he learns his lesson the hard way in a state training school
with all its rigors. We found that this rule does not always hold true.
Thereby hangs a complicated analysis.

In Columbus, the court had four choices of disposition: incarceration in a facility of the Ohio Youth Commission; confinement
in a juvenile detention center or, for older youths, sometimes in a
local jail; formal supervision by the Franklin County Probation Department; and "informal supervision," a term that calls for some not
very illuminating explanation. Usually, boys and girls who were
classed as receiving "informal supervision" got off with a reprimand
from the court with no further supervision at all. Sometimes there
was some surveillance by the police, and, rarely, assignment might
be made to a social service agency.

Our question was this: What effect did these differing dispositions have on the recidivism of our cohort? To arrive at an answer
several steps had to be taken. We distributed the dispositions by
offense category, as shown in table 3–6. It was surprising to find that
formal probation was so infrequently used with this group of delinquents. Assignment to probation occurred about as often as commitment to a state facility or to detention. By far the most frequently
used intervention was "informal supervision." As I have noted above,
this class of intervention was in reality nonintervention, though not
quite in the sense advocated by Schur.[17] Also notable in this table
is the heavier use of institutional penalties for the aggravated crimes
against the person. In spite of the gravity of the offenses falling in
this category, the court discriminated some offenders who, for various reasons, were not incarcerated. The primary reason was the
offender's tender years, as table 3–7 suggests.

The first point to be borne in mind while inspecting this table
is that the numbers represent arrests, not individuals. Thus there
were thirteen boys under age 13 who were committed to the Ohio
Youth Commission. These boys had been arrested for a total of eighty-
one offenses among them. Generalizing about this table, the first
finding to emerge is that the older the offender, the more likely it
will be that he will be sent to a training school: Slightly more than

Table 3–7
Distribution of Dispositions by Age of Arrested Juveniles at the Time of Arrest
(entire cohort, N = 1,222, 4,841 arrests)

Disposition	6 to 13	14 to 15	16 or older	Total
Institutional commitments				
Number	81	269	446	796
Percentage	5.5	15.8	26.8	16.4
Jail or detention				
Number	199	232	237	668
Percentage	13.5	13.6	14.2	13.8
Formal supervision				
Number	282	274	189	745
Percentage	19.1	16.1	11.3	15.4
Informal supervision				
Number	623	467	423	1,513
Percentage	42.3	27.4	25.4	31.3
Incomplete (disposition pending, unknown, or "other")				
Number	130	140	111	381
Percentage	8.8	8.2	6.7	7.9
Dismissed (includes "complaint withdrawn," and not guilty)				
Number	158	321	259	738
Percentage	10.7	18.9	15.6	15.2
Totals				
Number	1,473	1,703	1,665	4,481
Percentage	99.9[a]	100.0	100.0	100.0

Source: Federation for Community Planning, Cleveland, Ohio.
[a]Rounding error.

half of the oldest age group in our 1956 to 1958 subset were locked up. Conversely, over three-quarters of the age 6 to 13 bracket received some form of community supervision—or, as I have remarked above, nonintervention. These results were to be expected. One discovery that I find difficult to interpret is the fate of the thirteen preadolescents who landed in the care of the Ohio Youth Commission. All of them eventually were sentenced to prison. Was the juvenile court so prescient that a judgment was made that these were children who could already be predicted to be future career delinquents? Or was the decision to send them to a training school the critical event that confirmed them in delinquency?

Once again, a statistical sweep uncovers a problem that statistical methods cannot solve—this time, a problem of considerable

urgency. The inclination to apply the hard line to the juvenile offender is easy to extend to the very young. For all I can say here,
there may have been nothing else the court could have done with
respect to these thirteen boys: Nature had to take its course. But
that attitude accepts defeat too readily. Their subsequent fate surely
establishes that if assignment to a training facility did no harm, it
certainly did not do enough good to spare them and the Ohio tax-
payers the burden of long-term incarceration. Clearly, with respect
to this youngest group of offenders, there must be a clinical study
of the reasons for commitment in the first place, the nature of the
treatment administered in the training school, and the longitudinal
course of the ensuring delinquencies.

No variable, other than the nature of the offense itself, affected
disposition as much as the age of the offender. Race had some effect:
Blacks were a little more likely to be sent to institutions than whites
(40.7 percent of the blacks, 35.0 percent of the whites). The courts
dealt more leniently with girls than with boys: 38.7 percent of the
boys were locked up, against 31.9 percent of the girls, a contrast that
is at least in part attributable to the more serious nature of the boys'
offenses.

Having some idea of the dimensions of the variables for which
we had to control, we were now ready for the crucial question: How
much difference did the differing disposition make in the recidivism
of these offenders? The answer is seen in table 3–8. This table contains the most important single finding of our study. "Street time,"
as we defined the term, was the interval between release from custody in the case of an institutional commitment, or adjudication,
when the delinquent was assigned to community supervision. In all
categories of delinquents, street time was *less* after institutionalization than after any other disposition, in most cases much less than
the grand mean.

The significance of this finding is open to two contrasting, but
not incompatible, interpretations. We may infer that the institutional experience is so destructive that the offender's hostility is
enhanced to the point of indifference to the consequences of his
conduct. Although this is an all too probable result of commitment
to a training school, it must be recognized that the individuals chosen
for commitment to an institution are the worst risks, those who
must be expected to be the most likely to recidivate. *What is certain
from this finding is that the impact of a few months of confinement
has no decelerating effect on the rate at which new offenses will be
committed.*

Here we are at odds with the widely heralded conclusions of

Table 3–8
Net Mean Street Time (in Months) between Arrests by Type and Disposition of First Arrest in All Pairs of Arrests

(total cohort; all dispositions, N = 3553; grand mean, 917 months' street time)[a]

Disposition	Index Violence		Property Offenses		Assault		Other		Totals	
	N	Mean Street Time (months)	N	Mean Street Time (months)	N	Mean Street Time (months)	N	Mean Street Time (months)	N	Mean Street Time (months)
Institution	104	5.32	214	4.76	15	5.32	126	4.30	459	4.77
Jail-detention	40	8.38	162	8.93	46	11.17	240	7.16	488	8.23
Formal supervision	64	14.26	258	8.05	64	12.45	192	7.46	578	9.03
Informal supervision	65	15.54	388	13.27	118	18.46	624	9.56	1305	10.96
Incomplete[b]	35	13.47	97	8.44	16	12.19	159	7.75	307	8.85
Dismissed[c]	114	8.15	198	6.83	68	13.47	146	6.57	526	7.90

Source: Federation for Community Planning, Cleveland, Ohio.

[a]Grand mean, excluding incomplete and dismissed cases: 9.49 months.

[b]Disposition pending, unknown, or "other."

[c]Complaint withdrawn or not guilty verdict.

studies conducted by Murray of the American Institutes of Research.[18] In his evaluation of the Unified Delinquency Intervention Services of Chicago (UDIS), Murray assembled data leading to the generalization that institutional commitments tend to "suppress" delinquent behavior. Murray's statistical methods and conceptualization of the problem have been vigorously challenged by several reviewers, most recently by Burton of Applied Management Sciences.[19]

We are confident of the integrity of our findings so far as our data will take us. What is needed to resolve the difference between the two viewpoints is a close examination, case by case, of the experience of delinquents like ours during the street time between release or adjudication and the next offense. No doubt Murray's notion of "suppression" operates on some recidivists, but our data clearly show that it has little effect on the majority. Even where suppression is a factor, other factors must also be at work—a good job, a different neighborhood, a girlfriend who won't stand for hustling, or other pieces of good luck.

Proceeding further with the "velocity" of recidivism, we found that the intervals between each pair of offenses committed by the cohort members diminished as a delinquent career progressed. For the first five pairs of arrests, the average street time was 10.94 months, for arrests 5 to 10 the average was 5.47 months, for arrests 10 to 15 the average was 3.68 months, for arrests 15 to 12, 2.24 months.

This is a gloomy finding. It expresses in arithmetical terms the process of "hardening" delinquents. After they are caught up as clients of juvenile justice, the probability of apprehension and its consequences holds no further terrors. Many of these recidivists were rearrested within weeks of their release from an Ohio Youth Commission facility. No clairvoyance is required to foresee the ugly future ahead for these youths.

Summing Up

One outstanding conclusion to be drawn from our study of the violent few is the demonstration of the limitations of statistics as a guide to policy and decisions. Statistical analysis can shake confidence in the "common-sense" notions about the control of delinquency. In the Dangerous Offender Project we are repeatedly reminded that in the world outlook of the delinquent boy or girl common sense does not dominate. But statistical analysis is not helpful in discriminating the intangibles that decide individual successes and failures.

Some chronic offenders are "monster boys" (though we cannot be sure that we discovered any in our cohort), about whom no one knows what to do—except to provide for their prolonged sequestration. Other chronic offenders are relatively harmless nuisances who can be managed in the community, given the resources for constructive case management. Some violent children commit their violence early in their careers, for others a violent offense seems to be the culmination of careers devoted to lesser delinquencies.

Where rules for guidance are so often found inapplicable, it is not surprising that reliable predictions cannot be made about the future conduct of any delinquent—except for that minority of persisters, indifferent to anything the system can threaten or impose on them. This indifference is fully displayed in our study of the velocity of recidivism. The only aim clearly accomplished by the incarceration of the violent recidivist is temporary incapacitation.

Knowing many of the key figures in Columbus's juvenile justice system, I do not doubt their professionalism. In making their fateful decisions they genuinely hope to contribute to the best future possible for the unpromising boys and girls with whom they must deal. These decisions must be consistent with their sense of responsibility to the community. They are caught up in a system that is gravely defective, even allowing for influences beyond the reach of the system.

The condition is not local. Every major city in the country is affected by a juvenile justice system that staggers with overloading and carries on with concepts that are obsolete and invalid. The worst consequences are to be seen in the increase of a class of career adult criminals. The search for remedies to this tragic and dangerous condition is haphazard and half-hearted. This country does not need to resign itself to crime as a chronically worsening social malady. There are potential remedies, some of them not difficult to apply.

Notes

1. For an account of trends toward more severity toward juvenile offenders, see Donna M. Hamparian et al., *Youth in Adult Courts: Between Two Worlds* (Columbus, Ohio: Academy for Contemporary Problems, 1982), 201–12.

2. Donna Martin Hamparian, Richard Schuster, Simon Dinitz, and John P. Conrad, *The Violent Few* (Lexington, Mass.: Lexington Books, 1978).

3. Marvin E. Wolfgang, Robert M. Figlio, and Thorsten Sellin, *Delinquency in a Birth Cohort* (Chicago: University of Chicago Press, 1972).

4. *Ibid.*, 27–52.

5. *Ibid.*, 169.

6. *Ibid.*, 250.

7. The total cohort comprised 1,032 boys and 190 girls. There were several differences in the findings for the girls and the boys. The most notable was the much larger number of girls who were arrested for one offense only, desisting thereafter: 48 percent of the girls were arrested only once as compared to 26.0 percent of the males who were arrested once only. See Hamparian et al., *Youth in Adult Courts*, 53.

8. Readers of Hamparian et al., *The Violent Few* will observe a discrepancy here. In our earlier report the total number of subjects for the five-year cohort was 1,138. Since its publication, a further review of the Columbus police files uncovered 86 additional persons arrested for violent acts who were born in the cohort years. Two cases were excluded because dispositions could not be found, thus bringing the total number of subjects to 1,222. *The Violent Few* also relied on an analysis of the subset of 811 individuals born during the years 1956–58 because those were the delinquents who would have attained their eighteenth birthday at the conclusion of our study. As we now have data for the completed delinquent careers of the whole cohort, as well as their subsequent criminal careers, I am presenting most of the analysis accordingly. Because the follow-up study could not include some of variables used in *The Violent Few*, I have had to rely on the original data in a few cases. Where this has been done, I have referred to the source.

9. Mark A. Peterson, Harriet B. Braiker, with Suzanne M. Polich, *Doing Crime: A Survey of California Prison Inmates* (Santa Monica: Rand Corporation, April 1980). The Rand Corporation has made a specialty of self-reported criminal histories. See also Jan M. Chaiken and Marcia R. Chaiken, *Varieties of Criminal Behavior* (August 1982). There are no comparable studies of self-reported delinquent careers, a lack that someone, surely, will some day fill.

10. Sheldon Glueck and Eleanor Glueck, *One Thousand Juvenile Delinquents* (Cambridge, Mass.: Harvard University Press, 1934).

11. Sheldon Glueck and Eleanor Glueck, *Unraveling Juvenile Delinquency* (New York: Commonwealth Fund, 1950), 287.

12. Malcolm W. Klein, "Offence Specialisation and Versatility among Juveniles," *British Journal of Criminology* 24 (2) (April 1984):182–94. It would be useful to have a companion study of treatment programs and intervention strategies that really make calculated use of the assumption that delinquent careers are specialized. Pending the publication of such an investigation, I must doubt that these assumptions in practitioners' minds are very influential in the design of modalities or even in the disposition of individual delinquents.

13. *Ibid.*, 191.

14. For a fuller account of the unusual history of this boy, see "The Importance of Being George: Unanswered Questions about the Dangerous

Juvenile Offender," in John P. Conrad and Simon Dinitz, *In Fear of Each Other* (Lexington, Mass.: Lexington Books, 1977), 13–20. Since the publication of that essay, "George" has attained the years of manhood but is unregenerate. At the last report he was serving time in a midwestern prison for an armed robbery.

15. I am indebted to Donna Hamparian and Judy Jacobson of the Federation for Community Planning of Cleveland for the follow-up data on the adult careers of this cohort. Their report, tentatively entitled *Violent Juvenile Offenders: Early Adult Careers,* is in preparation for publication in 1985.

16. Hamparian et al., *Youth in Adult Courts,* 133.

17. Edwin Schur, *Radical Non-Intervention: Rethinking the Delinquency Problem* (Englewood Cliffs, N.J.: Prentice-Hall, 1975).

18. Charles Murray, Doug Thomson, and Cindy Israel, *UDIS: De-institutionalizing the Chronic Juvenile Offender* (Washington, D.C.: American Institute of Research, 1978). See also Charles A. Murray and Louis A. Cox, *Beyond Probation: Juvenile Corrections and the Chronic Delinquent* (Beverly Hills: Sage Library of Social Research, 1979), 31–43.

19. Bob Burton, *Re-analysis of UDIS Data* (Silver Spring, Md.: Applied Management Sciences, 1980).

4
The Life-Cycle of the Career Thug

No one knows how many Americans have willfully committed a life-threatening act against another human being. It is a fair guess that however many they may be, these men and women who have grievously breached the bounds of accepted conduct constitute a small minority of the whole population. For some a violent act was an isolated incident, never to be repeated. For too many, violence becomes the way to a brief enjoyment of power and the satisfactions that come with it. Violence is woven into their careers, as distinctive a feature of their personalities as a tradesman's dexterity with tools or an artist's mastery of technique.

The impact of chronic violent offenders on the community is far out of proportion to their numbers. They are exceptional people, objects of dread to the urban public. Their bad reputations are enhanced by their strangeness. They do things that most people would never do and cannot understand. In spite of the efforts of the police to sweep them off the streets, they are in the community, indistinguishable in most respects from ordinary men and women, but unpredictably dangerous to law-abiding citizens.

For the last century criminologists have studied these unusual creatures; indeed, the existence of dangerous offenders is one of the principal reasons for the existence of our discipline. These efforts have not been crowned with great success. Neither the prevention nor the cure of violent crime has ensued from our studies. The more modest objective of improved control seems to be the most that we can expect to achieve.

From the beginning, our group in Columbus planned the Dangerous Offender Project as an opportunity to collect information that would enable criminal justice policy-makers to bring about more effective control of repetitively violent offenders. We thought that one way of approaching this goal would be through increasing knowledge of the criminal careers of men and women who commit violent crime. We decided on a retrospective study of a large sample of the persons who were arrested on charges of violent crime in Columbus. In this chapter, I shall recapitulate the findings of this research. As in the last chapter's review of our study of juvenile violent offenders, I shall restrict myself to the information necessary to understand the results of our research and their implications. Those who wish to review our enquiry in full detail are referred to our full report, *Careers of the Violent.*[1]

The Research Design

Our data foundation comprised all adult male offenders arrested for a violent offense in Columbus during the years 1950 to 1976. With the cooperation of the Columbus police department, we drew two random samples from the records of arrests during the years chosen for our survey. This was a period that preceded the modernization made possible by the computer. Two massive ledgers in longhand had been kept in which arrests were logged by identification bureau personnel. One ledger, the "robbery book," contained the robberies and attempted robberies; the other, the "MARS book" (constructing an acronym appropriate for its contents), contained all the murders, aggravated assaults, and forcible rapes.

From the MARS book, we took every second name in chronological order for a total of 967 names. The robbery book was much larger, we limited our sampling to every twentieth arrest, and that yielded 624 names. In our analysis we found it advisable to separate the two samples for some purposes and to aggregate the total of 1,591 individuals for other aspects of the study. We saw no point in attempting to weight the sample because of the differences in the offenses or in the size of the two subsamples. However, because of the long period of time that was covered, we did divide the sample into three age groups: persons born before 1920, of whom there were 234, those born between 1920 and 1939, of whom there were 727, and those born in 1940 and thereafter, of whom there were 630.[2] Our sample thus includes some men who are now long since dead or who have retired from their criminal careers, but also many who are still actively engaged in thuggery.

The Federal Bureau of Investigation made arrest histories available to us for each person in the sample. That provided us with a listing of all arrests across the country for each individual. The Columbus police department opens an individual file for each person arrested for a felony and records all subsequent arrests with full details of each charge for the duration of his career. We were allowed full access to these files for each member of our sample. We coded the date of each arrest, the offense charged, all information on the disposition by prosecutors and courts, as well as the usual demographic data on birth-dates, race, and marital status.

It was important to have a detailed perspective on each person's complete arrest history. We classified arrests in three categories: index-violent, non–index-violent, and nonviolent. We were able to determine the total number of arrests for each man, their character, and their spacing throughout his career. The use to which we put these data will be apparent later in this chapter.

With all this material in hand, we could analyze each criminal history to determine persistence in or desistance from crime. We could separate groups of offenders according to the transitional probability of another arrest—violent or nonviolent. I shall devote a good deal of attention to the important findings that transpired from the study of transitional probabilities.

Demographic Characteristics and Criminal Histories

Race

The total sample was distributed disproportionately by race: 43.5 percent of our subjects were white, 56.5 percent were nonwhite. The overrepresentation of racial minorities—in this case almost wholly black—is typical of studies of this kind. The population of Columbus in 1970 was 12.5 percent black, a larger fraction than in previous years. Various interpretations have been made of this tragic datum. I prefer the most parsimonious: Chronic unemployment of many, insecure employment of many more, and the poverty of most accounts for black criminality more reasonably than any other set of causes that have been hypothesized. Like all U.S. cities, Columbus is affected by racism and suffers the consequences.

Age

Our data could not include arrests of our subjects when they were still juveniles. Beyond a doubt, there were many who had extensive delinquent careers preceding their qualification as full-fledged adult criminals. The ages at which a subject committed the violent offense that made him eligible for our study ranged from 16 to 73 (with 20 who were over age 60, and 79 over age 50—showing that violence is not entirely a young man's game). But by far the largest age group ranged from 18 to 35: There were 1,205 in this category, with a mode of 90 individuals at age 22.

Sex

Although Columbus women sometimes commit violent crimes, they do so much more infrequently than men and with different motives and in different offense categories. To include them would muddle the data. We decided to defer a study of female violence to another time.

Drinking and Drugs

Police files are not reliable sources of information about the habits of persons arrested. Usually a notation is made about addiction or alcoholism only if these conditions were thought to be in some way related to the crime committed. It is significant that 33.2 percent of our people were said to have drinking problems and 14.8 percent had drug histories. It seemed certain that more of our men sought surcease in bottles and needles, but no one can say how many.

The Crimes They Committed

These 1,591 men were arrested on a total of 12,527 occasions, for an average of 7.9 arrests per offender. Blacks averaged 8 arrests; whites, 7.6. How large the number of uncleared crimes they committed may be is beyond our speculation. Every study of this subject indicates that the arrests are a minor fraction of the total number of crimes committed by any career criminal. We kept this axiom in mind, but we were unable to apply it to our data.

Of the total sample 80, or 5.0 percent, were arrested on one occasion only, necessarily on a charge of a violent crime. Everyone else was a recidivist, and some, we shall see were persistent indeed. At the extreme end of the continuum, 81 men amassed more than 20 arrests apiece, one of them reaching the impressive total of 48.[3]

The criterion for inclusion in our sample was at least one arrest for one violent crime, but our subjects were no specialists in violence. The percentage distribution of crimes charged against these offenders is shown in Table 4–1. The line for "all other charges" (26.8 percent) was distributed among 74 categories of offense, including such mis-

Table 4–1
Percentage Distribution of 12,527 Crimes Charged against
Members of Study Sample

Offense	Percentage
Criminal homicide	3.3
Rape	3.2
Robbery	9.5
Felonious assault	7.5
Other assaults	9.7
Arson	0.5
Possession of weapons	4.6
Burglary, break-enter	8.1
Larceny	7.2
Auto theft	3.6
Forgery, counterfeit, bad checks	2.9
Intoxication	5.5
Drug violations	2.3
Traffic offenses, driving under the influence	5.3
All other charges	26.8
Total	100.0

Source: Miller, Dinitz, and Conrad, *Careers of the Violent,* 64–65. Some similar charges, listed separately in the original table, have been consolidated.

demeanors as spitting (2 arrests), violations of the blue sky laws (1 arrest), and rabies quarantine violation (one arrest). Other arrests were much more serious: extortion, contributing to the delinquency of a minor (126 arrests), safecracking (3 arrests), and destruction of property (90 arrests).

The patternless careers of the men in both subsamples was consistent with all other studies of this kind. Excluding those with one arrest only (necessarily a violent offense), there were 111, or 7.0 percent of the total who limited themselves to crimes of violence. The MARS offenders averaged 7 arrests; the robbers, 9 arrests. Twenty percent of the total were arrested 5 or more times for a violent offense. Fifty-two percent were arrested 2 to 4 times for index and nonindex violent crimes combined. Limiting the count to *index* violent crimes only, 5 percent were arrested on 5 or more such charges, but 44 percent were arrested for 2 to 4 index charges.

These 1,591 offenders did not restrict themselves to violence but often used life-threatening means to obtain their ends. Violence was a tool of their trade, an essential characteristic of their careers. We must examine these careers as closely as we can if ways are to be found to divert young men from adopting them.

The Findings: Frequency of Arrests

As I have already noted, our sample consisted of men who committed only one offense and others who committed many, as many as 48. In table 4–2 the careers are summarized, and it will be seen that to understand the violent offender some preliminary distinctions must be made among those who commit few offenses and those who commit many. The largest group of offenders, 886 in all (55.6 percent of the sample), were clustered in a group the members of which were arrested from two to seven times, with a modal point at three arrests. After the third arrest, the number of offenders dwindled steadily. Only 81 went on to 20 or more arrests.

We divided the sample into three groups: those who were arrested only once, those who were arrested from 2 to 4 times, and those who were arrested 5 or more times.

Table 4–3 calls for some explanation. We used the classification

Table 4–2
Number and Percentage of Offenders Desisting from Crime after Each Last Arrest for Crimes of Any Type

Arrest Sequence Number	Number	Percentage	Cumulative Percentage
1	80	5.0	5.0
2	153	9.6	14.6
3	178	11.2	25.9
4	154	9.7	35.6
5	144	9.1	44.6
6	119	7.5	52.1
7	138	8.7	60.7
8	81	5.1	65.8
9	76	4.8	70.6
10	73	4.6	75.2
11	60	3.8	79.0
12	64	4.0	83.0
13	41	2.6	85.6
14	41	2.6	88.1
15	27	1.7	89.8
16	23	1.4	91.3
17	24	1.5	92.8
18	16	1.0	93.8
19	18	1.1	94.9
20	15	0.9	95.9
21 to 48	65	4.1	
	1591	100.0	

Source: Miller, Dinitz, and Conrad, *Careers of the Violent*, 76.

Table 4–3
Distribution of Total Sample
(N = 1951, by number of arrests for all offenses, violent index, violent non-index, and non-violent offenses; single, multiple, and chronic offenders)

Number of Arrests	Persons		Arrests	
	N	Percentage	N	Percentage
All Arrests				
1	80	5.0	80	0.6
2–4	485	30.5	1,456	11.6
5 or more	1,025	64.5	10,991	87.7
	1,591		12,527	
Violent Index Charges Only				
1	731	48.2	731	24.7
2–4	709	46.7	1,778	60.0
5 or more	77	5.1	454	15.3
	1,517		2,963	
Non-Index Violent Charges Only				
1	440	49.1	440	21.8
2–4	362	40.4	941	46.6
5 or more	95	10.6	637	31.6
	897		2,018	
Nonviolent Charges Only				
1	144	11.1	257	3.4
2–4	529	41.0	1,532	20.3
5 or more	620	48.0	5,757	76.3
	1,293		7,546	

Source: Miller, Dinitz, and Conrad, *Careers of the Violent*, 78.

of recidivism introduced by Wolfgang, Figlio and Sellin in their *Delinquency in a Birth Cohort*, to which frequent allusion was made in chapter 3.[4] It will be seen that our sample consisted of a majority of chronic offenders—64.5 percent of the total—who committed 87.7 percent of all the offenses charged to our subjects. This figure is disturbing on the face of it, but when we proceed down the table we discover that while these men were inveterate criminals, relatively few were *chronically violent*. Only 5.1 percent committed five or more violent index offenses, only 10.6 percent of those who committed nonindex violent offenses committed five or more of them. Nevertheless the chronic offenders in each category, violent or nonviolent, accounted for far more than their share of the offenses committed.

The Persistence of the Criminal Careerist

Both our MARS offenders and our robbers were impressively persistent in the commission of a wide variety of felonies and misdemeanors. Though it might be thought that the MARS men would be less persistent than the robbers—simply because their crimes were "expressive" rather than "instrumental"—it turned out that they were arrested for a wide assortment of nonexpressive crimes. Many of them matched the robbers in the length and severity of their criminal records. A tentative inference is suggested: *Once a disposition to commit violence is established, the barriers to the violation of other laws are lowered or disappear.*

In table 4–4 we see the persistence of criminality so far as statistics can represent it. Ninety-five percent of our subjects continued to commit some kind of crime after their first arrests, and desistance was slow indeed. Not until the sixth arrest had as many as half our men desisted from further offenses. In column 7 the probability that members of the group arrested for any ordinal number of arrests would proceed to another is calculated. We were impressed that until the end of this long sequence the transitional probability of another offense is far better than even.

At first glance, this extraordinary level of persistence would seem to justify a strategy of incapacitation. These are recidivists who are not to be deterred by any action by the criminal justice system against them. When they can, they will return to some kind of criminal activity. But it must be kept in mind that, as we saw in table 4–1, 42.9 percent of the arrests were for minor charges including intoxication (693), disorderly conduct (222), suspicion (260), technical parole violations (355), and traffic offenses (469). All of these charges and many more on the list are short of the conduct expected of good citizens, but hardly require incarcerative restraint. The persistence of violence defines the dangerous offender.

In table 4–5 we limit our scrutiny of desistance and persistence to violent crimes only. Our interest is the crucial question, What are the probabilities that offenders who have committed one index violent crime will commit more? To the extent that dangerousness can be statistically defined, these probabilities measure it. The offenses represented in this table are all serious, all potentially life-threatening. They contrast strongly with the relatively trivial charges included in table 4–4.. Yet over half those who committed a violent offense committed another when they could, and the transitional probabilities among the recidivists continue well above 40 percent. To derive a guide to policy from these data is a puzzle, but the

Table 4–4
Desistance, Persistence, and Transitional Probability of Committing Any Crime after Each Arrest
(total sample, N = 1,591)

Number of Arrests	Number of Subjects at Each Arrest	Number Desisting	Percentage Desisting	Number Persisting	Percentage Persisting	Transitional Probabilities
1	1591	80	5.0	1511	95.0	95.0
2	1511	153	9.6	1358	85.4	89.9
3	1358	178	11.2	1180	74.2	86.9
4	1180	154	9.7	1026	64.5	87.0
5	1026	144	9.1	882	55.4	86.0
6	882	119	7.5	763	48.0	86.5
7	763	138	8.7	625	39.3	81.5
8	625	81	5.1	544	34.2	87.0
9	544	76	4.8	468	29.4	86.0
10	468	73	4.6	395	24.8	84.4
11	395	60	3.8	335	21.1	84.8
12	335	64	4.0	271	17.0	80.9
13	271	41	2.6	230	14.5	84.9
14	230	41	2.6	189	11.9	82.2
15	189	27	1.7	162	10.2	85.7
16	162	23	1.5	139	8.7	85.8
17	139	24	1.5	115	7.2	82.7
18	115	16	1.0	99	6.2	86.1
19	99	18	1.1	81	5.1	81.8
20	81	15	0.9	66	4.2	81.5
21	66	7	0.4	59	3.7	89.4
22	59	6	0.4	53	3.3	89.8
23	53	1	0.1	52	3.3	98.1
24	52	7	0.4	45	2.8	86.5
25	45	4	0.3	41	2.6	91.1
26	41	6	0.4	35	2.2	85.4

Table 4–4 (continued)
Desistance, Persistence, and Transitional Probability of Committing Any Crime after Each Arrest
(total sample, N = 1,591)

Number of Arrests	Number of Subjects at Each Arrest	Number Desisting	Percentage Desisting	Number Persisting	Percentage Persisting	Transitional Probabilities
27	35	7	0.4	28	1.8	80.0
28	28	7	0.4	21	1.3	75.0
29	21	3	0.2	18	1.1	85.7
30	18	1	0.1	17	1.1	94.4
31	17	3	0.2	14	0.9	82.4
32	14	2	0.1	12	0.8	82.4
33	12	1	0.1	11	0.7	85.7
34	11	1	0.1	10	0.6	90.9
38	10	1	0.1	9	0.6	90.0
40	9	2	0.1	7	0.4	77.8
41	7	1	0.1	6	0.4	85.7
42	6	1	0.1	5	0.3	83.3
45	5	2	0.1	3	0.2	60.0
46	3	2	0.1	1	0.1	33.3
48	1	1	0.1	—	—	—

Source: Miller, Dinitz, and Conrad, Careers of the Violent, 71–72.

Table 4–5
Desistance, Persistence, and Transitional Probability of Committing a Violent Crime after Each Arrest for a Violent Crime
(all subjects arrested for index violence; N = 1,517)

Number of Arrests	Number of Subjects at Each Arrest	Number Desisting	Percentage Desisting	Number Persisting	Percentage Persisting	Transitional Probabilities
1	1,517	731	48.1	786	51.8	51.8
2	786	438	28.9	348	22.9	44.3
3	348	182	12.0	166	10.9	47.7
4	166	89	5.9	77	5.1	46.4
5	77	41	2.7	36	2.4	46.8
6	36	18	1.2	18	1.2	50.0
7	18	13	0.9	5	0.3	27.8
8	5	1	0.1	4	0.3	80.0
9	4	2	0.1	2	0.1	50.0
10	2	1	0.1	1	0.1	50.0
14	1	1	0.1	—	—	—

Source: Miller, Dinitz, and Conrad, *Careers of the Violent*, 66.

indication that restraint is needed is clear. I shall return to this perplexity in chapter 7. Its resolution depends on the digestion of more data.

The Limits to Generalization

We had to depend on the FBI's arrest histories, which form the data bank for the *Uniform Crime Reports.* Realism requires that reservations of two kinds must be made in any study that makes such extensive use of these indispensable statistical collections. They are vulnerable on two general counts. First, some police departments, for strategic reasons of their own, will underreport or overreport the crimes committed in their jurisdictions. The FBI cannot make thorough audits of their reports. We are confident of the accuracy of the contemporary Columbus reports but could not assure that reporting practices did not differ with personnel changes from time to time over the twenty-five years of our study. We are less sure of the entries in arrest histories submitted—or not submitted—by other police departments in other cities. Some of our subjects were widely traveled men.

Second, and more serious, is the "dark side" of criminal statistics. Victimization surveys and self-reported criminal histories have repeatedly shown that many crimes never come to police attention and even more are never cleared. The number varies with the nature of the crime. Few murders go unreported, but many assaults, forcible rapes, and robberies are kept quiet for various reasons: fear of retaliation, embarrassment, lack of confidence in the police, and—sometimes—a reconciliation between the victim and the offender. I do not doubt that many of these unknown offenses were committed by the men of our sample, but I must refrain from speculation in the absence of data affording me the slightest basis for estimate.

Still another problem is the interpretation of our results in the light of negotiated justice. In our study, 6,500, or 51.9 percent of the 12,527 offenses resulted in a guilty verdict on some charge, but often not the charge made by the police. There were 130 acquittals and 5 verdicts of not guilty by reason of insanity, or 1 percent. Charges were dismissed in 18.8 percent of the cases. There was no way to determine the outcome in the remaining 28.3 percent, but we estimated that a large share of this fraction consisted of men on whom the county prosecutor pled *nolle prosequi.* That plea never stands as an ornament to the system as a whole. Either the police arrested the wrong man or could not provide enough evidence to support the charge—or the prosecutor declined to proceed because he or she feared to lose the case.

Throughout our study and this summary, the data are presented as though each arrest represented the offense recorded by the police. I will defend this practice as the best we could do to make a consistent picture of the reality of the crimes committed. Certainly there were more crimes, and certainly, negotiated justice being what it is, the crimes charged by the police were filed at the most serious level consistent with the facts. Sometimes the charge was reduced because of the county prosecutor's professional determination that the facts submitted by the police did not support the charge. Sometimes, the prosecutor would make a deal with the defendant to reduce the charge to remove the case from the docket, even though the facts would have clearly supported the original charge. The number of acquittals and the dismissed charges indicate that at least some of our sample did not commit the offenses with which they were charged. A very small minority of the entire sample—80, or 5 percent of the total—had only one entry on their records. It is reasonable to suppose that the number of offenders and the offenses that we have reported substantially understates the numbers of violent offenders in Columbus and the mischief for which they were responsible during the years of our study.

Having faced up to these inadequacies and acknowledged the gap between reality and official records, I claim that all signs point to a situation more serious than is reflected in our statistics. The data show a high rate of persistence in known criminal activity, even allowing for the numerous arrests for minor offenses that appear in the records of our sample. Persistence in the commission of unknown offenses must have been comparable in number to those that were recorded. Well-known police characters do not get away with many major crimes, but their hustles and muggings go on just the same, adding to the fears and apprehensions of their fellow-citizens.

Nevertheless, there was a perceptible rate of desistance about which we can only speculate. Some of these men died while still engaged in their careers. Some must have been intimidated by their experiences with the police, the courts, and the jails. Some were locked up for so long that more crime was out of the question. Some may have been rehabilitated. Some were lucky in getting a good job or marrying a good wife. Nevertheless the desistance rate hovered at the level of 10 percent from the second to the fifth arrests. The chances should be best for dissuading an offender from pursuing his career during the early stages, but our subjects were not often convinced.

Age and Violent Careers

It is a truism that violent crime comes most easily to young men. Our data verify this hoary axiom; indeed, we might have said that the consistency of our findings with the axiom confirms their validity. The data further support the corollary that the younger a boy is when his name first appears in a register of arrests the longer his career will be. Note that this finding is based only on the records of adult arrests. Keeping in mind our conclusions on violent juvenile offenders in chapter 3, we do not doubt that if we had had access to the juvenile arrest records of these 1,591 adult offenders, this relationship between the age of onset and the duration of the full criminal career would be even more pronounced.

That conclusion will cause no surprise to informed practitioners. Anyone who has worked in police stations, prosecutors' offices, or prison reception centers will be well aware of the long and dreary records young offenders bring with them and the seeming impossibility of extricating most of them from the hopeless trouble they choose or into which they drift in spite of professed good intentions.

What is more disturbing is our finding that so many of our offenders continued their criminal activities for so long. The conventional belief is that crime is a young man's fancy. It is thought that as middle age approaches the excitement palls, the energy that propels a man into making a score diminishes, and the criminal begins to consider another and more conventional occupation. With our subjects, careers did not "burn out" as soon as would be expected. In our total sample, 710 (44.6 percent) were last arrested *after* the age of 35, 318 (20 percent) were arrested for the last time *after* the age of 45. In a sense, these figures are preliminary; many of our men had not reached the age of 35 by the time we closed the books on this study. It was moderately encouraging to note that the robbers seemed to be the first to yield to advancing age. Whereas 23.4 percent of the MARS sample was still actively engaged in crime after age 45, only 14.7 percent of the robbers were still plying their trade at that age.

So much for our sample as a collection of generalists in crime. When we narrow the focus to violent crime, the perspective is surprising. As shown in table 4–6, there was a substantial number of middle-aged MARS offenders and robbers who persisted in index violent crime. Of the MARS subsample, 357 (38.2 percent) committed their *last* violent crime after age 35. The robbers were much less

Table 4–6
Distribution of 935 MARS Offenders and 582 Robbers by Age at Last Arrest for Index Violent Offense

	MARS Offenders			Robbers		
Age	N	Percentage	Cumulative Percentage	N	Percentage	Cumulative Percentage
15–19	59	6.3	6.3	60	10.3	10.3
20–24	178	19.0	25.3	172	29.6	39.9
25–29	168	18.0	43.3	140	24.1	64.0
30–34	173	18.5	61.8	94	16.2	80.2
35–39	129	13.8	75.6	49	8.4	88.6
40–44	91	9.7	85.3	28	4.8	93.4
45–49	59	6.3	91.6	22	3.8	97.2
50–54	35	3.7	95.3	13	2.2	99.4
55 and older	43	4.6	99.9	4	0.7	101.1
Total:	935	99.9		582	100.1	

Source: Dangerous Offender Project data file.

Table 4–7
Distribution of 517 MARS Offenders and 380 Robbers by Age of Last Arrest for a Non-Index Violent Offense

	MARS Offenders			Robbers		
Age	N	Percentage	Cumulative Percentage	N	Percentage	Cumulative Percentage
10–14	1	0.2	0.2	1	0.3	0.3
15–19	28	5.4	5.6	28	7.4	7.7
20–24	104	20.1	25.7	101	26.6	34.3
25–29	97	18.8	44.5	78	20.5	54.8
30–34	82	15.9	60.4	61	16.1	70.9
35–39	72	13.9	74.3	36	9.5	80.4
40–44	52	10.1	84.4	35	9.2	89.6
45–49	38	7.4	91.8	20	5.3	94.9
50–54	26	5.0	96.8	12	3.2	98.1
55 and older	17	3.3	100.1	8	2.1	100.2
Total:	517	100.1		380	100.2	

Source: Dangerous Offender Project data file.

persistent, but 116 (18.8 percent) committed their last violent offense after age 35.

For comparison, Table 4–7 shows the persistence of the two

subsamples in the commission of non-index violent offenses. Fewer of these offenses were committed, but the distribution by age groups is not strikingly different.

Data Trends from Generation to Generation

When we compared the three generations of offenders that we arbitrarily defined for the analysis, some differences stood out. The men born before 1920 received the heaviest sentences for violent charges; the two succeeding generations were less severely sentenced. The earlier two generations were incarcerated for a longer average time than the men born between 1940 and 1959, but their longer sentences did not shorten their persistence in criminal careers.

The youngest age group, those born in 1940 and later, is still criminally active. If our analysis of the rate of arrests so far is correct, this youngest group will average at least ten arrests apiece at the conclusion of their careers. Our guess is consistent with the commonly held opinion that the present generation of criminals is more recalcitrant than the offender of earlier days.

Social pessimists should not invest too heavily in this conclusion. It is also probable that at least some of the intergenerational difference may be attributed to increased police efficiency. More offenders are caught and investigations are more thorough. One would expect that this factor should be statistically reflected in the data in view of the large social and economic expenditures that have been allocated toward that end.

Dispositions

In this chapter we have considered the most feared criminals with whom the administration of justice must cope. It is important here to consider what happened to them once they were arrested, found guilty, and sentenced. The criminal justice system exists to respond to crime; we need to know how effective that response is to the kinds of crimes that citizens most wish to prevent.

Our 1,591 men were arrested on 12,527 occasions. They were found guilty in 6,500 cases. The sentence was probation in 1,942 cases; confinement or the death penalty in 4,421 instances. In only 1,849 cases did the sentence exceed one year, including three who were sentenced to death. Our violent men were often charged with much less serious offenses, all of which were duly recorded. In a crowded system, misdemeanors are often overlooked, even when committed by men whose appetite for serious crime is well known.

Limiting the analysis to the violent offenses that qualified these offenders for our scrutiny, we found that for these 1,591 offenses 988 men served terms of less than one year, 247 served a year, 218 were sentenced to terms of less than ten years, and 138 were sentenced to terms ranging from ten years to life.

Examining all index violent-offense dispositions, we found that 59 percent of the MARS offenders and 69.2 percent of the robbers received prison or jail sentences for their first offense. As records lengthened, conviction and a long term of imprisonment became more certain. Young men were also awarded longer terms in prison. We noted that age 22 may be the best time of life—except when facing a judge for sentencing.

Nothing in our data suggested that the courts discriminated against blacks in sentencing decisions. Once a man is enmeshed in the criminal justice system, his status as an offender is far more significant than his race. This finding holds true for the entire sample going back to the 1950s when it might have been supposed that judges and prosecutors would have been less sensitive to charges of racial bias.

The Velocity of Crime

In chapter 3 I reviewed our investigation of the "velocity" of careers in juvenile delinquency. We applied the same strategy to our study of adult violent offenders. As with the juvenile birth cohorts, we measured the time between each pair of arrests for each offender, arriving at the *calendar time* between arrests. We also measured the time spent in custody, which we were able to obtain for only 18 percent of the paired arrests. This lack was technically unfortunate. If we had been able to determine the time in custody for each arrest, we would have been able to measure the actual *street time* for each offender. We did compare the street time with the calendar time when we could. The results were sufficiently consistent in tendency to justify the use of calendar time in measuring velocity.

We reasoned that if punishment had an effectively intimidating effect—the abstract, sanitized term is *specific deterrence*—on our men, the average time between arrests would increase as the years passed in the course of a criminal career. Conversely, if the average time between arrests decreased, the deterrent value of punishment would be of less value for the offenders under study. It is not unreasonable to infer that offenders who are released from jail or prison and are not re-convicted have been deterred, although other factors may also have influenced them. Those who are released but make a speedy return to crime certainly have not been deterred.

The complete analysis can be found in *Careers of the Violent* and will not be reproduced here. The conclusions were simple. In the early phases of their careers, the velocity of MARS offenders was somewhat slower than the robbers, but in later phases there was no significant difference. The time between arrests was marginally slower for offenders sentenced to prison than for those who did not receive incarcerative sentences.

Limiting our attention to index violence, we find that among the MARS offenders the average time between the first and second arrests on violent charges was 6.6 years, while the average calendar time for robbers was 5.4 years. As the arrests accumulated, this difference disappeared. The men who went on to their fourth arrests on index-violence charges averaged 4.4 years for MARS offenders and 4.6 years for robbers. For the relatively few who continued past that point the velocity increased to less than two years between "violent" arrests.

Summing up the findings from our study of velocity, three conclusions stand out: *First,* the longer the subject's record, the shorter will be the interval between arrests. *Second,* the velocity of arrests was faster in the early phases of long criminal careers. We put it that *high velocity at the beginning of a criminal career portends a long succession of contacts with the criminal justice apparatus. A rapid increase in the velocity of criminal acts at any point in an arrest history will indicate increased seriousness as well as increased frequency of violations. Third,* penal sanctions had a slight but measurable effect in retarding the velocity of a criminal career. In street time the average reduction after a severe incarcerative sentence was about 0.3 years. This delayed resumption of criminal careers will be difficult to balance against the cost of four months of incarceration.

Because of the unavoidable incompleteness of our data, these findings must be interpreted with caution. Their tendency suggests the potential usefulness of the calculation of street time if applied to a universe of offenders for whom complete data on criminal justice transactions is available.

In chapter 7 I shall return to our findings about the disposition of these violent men by the court. In the meantime, note that they tended to be dealt with rather leniently at first, perhaps reflecting a hope that they could be diverted from their criminal careers and perhaps showing that plea bargaining is a transaction that tends to favor the fledgling criminal.

No Monsters

From time to time mysterious circumstance produces a criminal monster, a man or woman whose violence is so persistent and so cruel that it grossly exceeds the criminality of the ordinary thug. No such person was found in our sample, although it is quite possible that during the long period covered by our study there may have been monsters on the ledgers. Our sampling missed them. In the MARS book our random procedures picked out only 40 of the 967 who had committed two or more index crimes against the person. When non-index violent crimes were added, this group grew to only 84. Among the robbers, there were only 9 out of the 624 who limited themselves to index crimes against the person; adding in the non-index violent crimes produced a total of 27. There were 111 of the total sample who were repetitively and exclusively violent. In only 6 homicide arrests was more than one murder charged.

Summary of Our Findings

In chapter 7 I will present the implications of our study of adult violent offenders. Here the main findings deserve a recapitulation:

1. Of the total of 1,591 men in the sample, 420 (26.7 percent) committed only one offense, necessarily violent. The rest—1171 (73.3 percent)—were recidivists.
2. Recidivists will commit more violent crimes: The "transitional probability" of another offense is about 80 percent. The chance that a recidivist will commit another violent offense is about fifty–fifty.
3. The data accumulated do not support a proposition that the criminal justice system can or does deter recidivist violent offenders. The substantial number of men (slightly more than a quarter) who committed one and only one offense indicates that the best chance of deterrence is at the outset of a criminal career. It is worth noting—though of what significance I cannot say—

that of the 63 once-only MARS men, 57.1 percent were sentenced to prison, of the 17 once-only robbers, 58.8 percent were sent to prison. Recidivists were indifferent to the consequences administered by the criminal justice system. On their subsequent offenses, which may have been lesser charges, prison sentences were imposed on a minority, often less than 20 percent.
4. None of the statistical variables we could use, alone or in combination, was a successful predictor of dispositions. This unpredictability is most plausibly attributed to the broad discretion allowed judges and prosecutors.

Columbus is a well-managed city, but it is not Utopia. Like all major U.S. cities, it benefits from the cultural and ethnic pluralism that is a source of great vitality to the nation. But pluralism is also a source of conflict and inequality. The twenty-five years of our study covered a period of sharp and often bitter strife from which Columbus was not immune. Under these circumstances, it could not have been expected that the city would be free of serious crime problems. By hindsight, it is clear that these problems could have been better controlled. The best use of hindsight is to use it for the sake of a better future.

Notes

1. Stuart J. Miller, Simon Dinitz, and John P. Conrad, *Careers of the Violent* (Lexington, Mass.: Lexington Books, 1982).
2. *Ibid.*, 41–42.
3. Considering the triviality of many of the charges against our recidivists, this is hardly surprising. All the charges against the once-only offenders were for violent offenses. Many of the charges against the recidivists were misdemeanors, not qualifying them for a return to prison.
4. Marvin E. Wolfgang, Robert M. Figlio, and Thorsten Sellin, *Delinquency in a Birth Cohort* (Chicago, The University of Chicago Press, 1972), pp. 65–87.

5
Reducing Crime by Restraining the Criminal: The Cost of the Cure

One of the most thoughtful proponents of the hard line in criminal justice is James Q. Wilson, whose book, *Thinking About Crime*, has been an influential statement in favor of increased use of incarceration to prevent the "safety crimes."[1] The final paragraph of this volume inspired our investigation of incapacitation as the objective of sentencing:

> Intellectuals, although they often dislike the common person as an individual, do not wish to be caught saying uncomplimentary things about humankind. Nevertheless, some persons will shun crime even if we do nothing to deter them, while others will seek it out even if we do everything to reform them. Wicked people exist. Nothing avails except to set them apart from innocent people. And many people, neither wicked nor innocent, but watchful, dissembling, and calculating of their opportunities, ponder our reaction to wickedness as a cue to what they might profitably do. We have trifled with the wicked, made sport of the innocent, and encouraged the calculators. Justice suffers, and so do we all.[2]

Coming from a distinguished Harvard professor, Wilson's disdain for intellectuals is difficult to explain. Nevertheless, so far as it goes, this paragraph was and still is an accurate account of the predicament of U.S. criminal justice. Obviously, the half-hearted commitment of the system to the rehabilitation of criminals has been worn thread-bare. Oratory and anecdotes have never filled the gap between professed aspirations and negligible achievements. As for the notion that if prisons don't rehabilitate, at least they deter criminals from continuing their careers, there is no serious evidence that recidivists—the most feared criminals—are intimidated by the sanctions of the penal codes. Wilson's view that they must be "set apart" for the protection of law-abiding citizens frankly opened up discourse on incapacitation. If criminal careerists can be locked up for long enough, how much crime would thereby be prevented? And how long would "long enough" be?

With these questions in mind, we decided to see what the answers might look like if we used Columbus, our home base, as a statistical laboratory. We wanted to find out how much violent crime would be prevented if the courts locked up career felons whenever possible. As matters stand in the administration of criminal justice, many criminals remain in the community after their arrest and trial on the charges against them—sometimes on probation, sometimes because the police have not marshaled enough evidence for a successful prosecution, and sometimes because of an acquittal or dismissal of charges. Suppose that all felons were to be securely set apart in a state prison?

We reasoned that in a statistical experiment we could assume that all persons arrested on charges of a violent crime were in fact guilty. We could then see what would have happened had each violent felon been sentenced to an *incapacitating* term in prison after the last previous conviction on a felony charge. In short, how many wicked felons could be set apart from the innocent? In setting them apart, to what extent would the innocent be protected from violent crime?

The Research Design

We chose the calendar year 1973—two years before the beginning of our project—as the base period for our investigation. Our fundamental question was, How many of the violent crimes that were committed during that year would have been prevented had those who committed them been incarcerated as a consequence of their last previous conviction?

Some basic data were readily available. During that year, 2,892 index crimes of violence were reported to the 28 reporting police departments in Franklin County. Of this number 638 were cleared by arrests of 342 adults: 337 men and 5 women. An additional 154 offenses were cleared by the arrest of 126 juveniles. We had a total of 792 offenses cleared—27.4 percent of the 2,892 crimes for which we wanted to account. The percentages of clearances varied considerably, as will be seen in tables 5–1 and 5–2.

The situation presented in table 5–1 is not unusual. Police clearance rates are low throughout the country for the stranger-to-stranger

Table 5–1
Total Recorded Violent Offenses and Violent Offenses Cleared, Franklin County, Ohio, 1973

Offense	Reported Violent Index Crimes, 1973	Cleared by Arrest		Cleared by Conviction	
		Number	Percentage of Index Crimes	Number	Percentage of Index Crimes
Murder/ manslaughter	65	62	95.4	34	52.3
Robbery	1,554	324	20.8	120	7.7
Sex offenses (violent)	326	143	43.9	29	8.9
Assault	947	109	11.5	48	5.1
Totals	2,892	638	22.1	231	8.0

Source: Van Dine, Conrad, and Dinitz, *Restraining the Wicked*, 61.

crimes. The even lower rate of conviction in court requires some elaborating detail. Of the 342 persons arrested by the police, 215 were finally convicted of a crime. Of the rest, 52 were "no billed" after a presentation to the Franklin County grand jury—that is, the jury refused to indict the individual arrested and charged. Another 44 were considered by the county prosecutor and given the benefit of a plea of *nolle prosequi* in the court of common pleas: The evidence was too shaky to support a successful prosecution. Four more were dismissed by a magistrate at the time of arraignment. Finally, 26 were acquitted after being brought to trial. In the one remaining case, we were unable to trace the disposition.

To complete the accounting for the known violent offenders we went to the records of the juvenile bureau of the Columbus police. For technical reasons it was not possible to secure the data from the Franklin County juvenile court, which would have given us all the juveniles who were arrested throughout the county. Instead we were limited to the juveniles arrested in Columbus, and the universe of violent offenses was reduced from 2,892 to the 2,622 crimes reported to the FBI by the city's police department. Table 5–2 shows the clearances by arrest and by conviction.

We decided to play the hard line. Although the data presented here indicate that the 342 adults arrested by the police included a substantial number who were not guilty, we wanted to make a maximum showing for severity in the experiment we proposed to conduct. If we made the outrageous assumption that the police always

Table 5–2
**Violent Offenses in Columbus Cleared by Juvenile Arrest and
Juvenile Conviction in 1973**

Offense	Number Reported[a]	Cleared by Arrest		Cleared by Conviction	
		Number	Percentage of Index Crimes	Number	Percentage of Index Crimes
Murder/ manslaughter	64	2	3.1	1	1.6
Robbery	1508	111	7.4	74	4.9
Sex offenses (violent)	295	18	6.1	11	3.7
Assault	755	23	3.0	20	2.6
Totals	2622	154	5.9	106	4.0

[a]As shown in the *Uniform Crime Reports* (1973), table 75, p. 233.

arrested the right culprit and did not have to prove his guilt in court, to what extent would crime control be strengthened? We resolved all the arrests in favor of the police. All the persons arrested and charged were counted as guilty. We designated them all as *offenders* regardless of their disposition by the court.

The next question sent us into their criminal histories, the "rap sheets" accumulated by the police and the Federal Bureau of Investigation. We needed to know how many of these offenders had previous felony convictions during the five years preceding their arrest. Our objective was to discover the effectiveness of various hypoethical sentencing policies in preventing the 638 crimes that our 342 offenders were presumed to have committed. We laid out and tested 16 such policies.[3] As to each policy, the same question was asked and answered: Given this offender's felony history, could his 1973 violent offense have been prevented by the application of this policy at the time of his previous conviction, if any?

The Findings

The most severe of our hypothetical policies, which we designated as *Policy 4*, called for five years' mandatory incarceration, without remission for "good time" or parole, on the conviction of *any* felony, regardless of status as to recidivism. Because this policy would incapacitate far more felons than any of our other hypothetical policies, we gave it the most detailed attention. The most lenient policy that we considered required a mandatory three-year term after a *third* felony conviction, with two prior convictions of violent felonies. I shall not burden this chapter with the results of our tests of each policy. A full account can be found in *Restraining the Wicked*.[3] Tables 5–3, 5–4, and 5–5 provide perspectives on the relative value of some representative policies as they would affect adult offenders, juvenile offenders, and both cohorts combined.

Table 5–3
The Impact of Five Sentencing Policies (Adult Cohort)

			Measure of Prevention			
Policy Number	Persons Prevented	Percentage of Cohort[a]	Indictment Charges Prevented	Percentage of all Violent Offenses[b]	Conviction Counts Prevented	Percentage of all Violent Offenses[b]
1	37	10.8	61	2.1	24	0.8
4	63	18.4	111	3.8	48	1.7
5	24	7.0	38	1.3	13	0.4
6	9	2.6	17	0.6	4	0.1
10	20	5.8	37	1.3	24	0.8

[a]The cohort of 342 offenders arrested.
[b]The total of 2,892 violent felonies in Franklin County in 1973.

Policy 1: One conviction, no prior violent felony, three-year mandatory sentence.
Policy 4: One conviction, no prior felony, five-year mandatory sentence.
Policy 5: Two convictions, no prior violent felony, five-year mandatory sentence.
Policy 6: Three convictions, no prior violent felony, five-year mandatory sentence.
Policy 10: One conviction, one violent felony required, five-year mandatory sentence.

Table 5–4
The Impact of Five Sentencing Policies (Juvenile Cohort)

	Juveniles Prevented		Counts Prevented (N = 2,622)			
Policy Number[a]	Persons Prevented	Percentage of Cohort[b]	Charges Prevented	Percentage of all Reported Crimes	Conviction Counts Prevented	Percentage of all Reported Crimes
1	28	22.2	30	1.1	23	0.9
4	33	26.2	35	1.3	27	1.0
5	14	11.1	14	0.5	13	0.5
6	6	4.8	6	0.2	5	0.2
10	11	8.7	11	0.4	10	0.4

[a]See table 5–3 for criteria for each policy.
[b]The cohort of 126 juveniles arrested for violent offenses in Columbus only during 1973.

Table 5–5
The Impact of Five Sentencing Policies (Combined Adult and Juvenile Cohorts)

Policy Number[a]	Persons Prevented		Arrest Counts		Conviction Counts	
	Number	Percentage[b]	Number	Percentage	Number	Percentage
1	78	16.7	116	4.0	59	2.0
4	96	20.5	210	7.3	105	3.6
5	77	16.5	135	4.7	62	2.1
6	48	10.3	77	2.7	35	1.2
10	49	10.5	78	2.7	49	1.7

[a]See table 5–3 for criteria for each policy.
[b]Percentage of combined cohorts, N = 468.

Policy 4, the most preventive of our hypothetical sanctions, calls for a degree of severity that surpasses the demands of any realistic hard-liner. It requires no exception to the rule that any person convicted of *any* felony must serve a flat term of five years in a state prison. The only crimes such a person could commit during his service of such a sentence would be those he might commit within the walls that confined him. No state penal statutes contain so sweeping and so rigorous a sanction. Given the enormous costs of incarceration, it is unlikely that any state will be so imprudent as to adopt it.

Yet of the violent crimes committed in Columbus in 1973, this severe legislation would have prevented a minimum of less than 8 percent—the 210 crimes committed by persons, adult or juvenile, previously convicted of a felony during the period 1968–73, that the police were able to clear. That is too restrictive an interpretation of our data. The 96 individuals whose crimes would have been thus forestalled surely committed other offenses for which they were not charged. How many more no one can know for sure, but there is good enough reason to assume that many more than the 210 crimes with which they were charged would have been prevented. Further, it must be kept in mind that Policy 4 would incapacitate many offenders who might have committed violent crimes for which they were not apprehended. Later in our analysis of the data we will have to take this likely contingency into our accounting. I will come back to this problem and to our estimates of the numbers of unattributed crimes that these offenders might have committed during their five years of liberty after their earlier conviction.

Meanwhile we must return to the data. Of the 342 adult offenders arrested by the police, 279 had not been convicted of a felony during the previous five years. That meant that the 1973 offenses for which they were taken into custody could not have been prevented by Policy 4. These individuals were charged with 527 offenses. Tracing the records of the violent juveniles, we found that 93 had no felony priors. These "virgins" were charged with 119 violent offenses, thereby making a total of 646 charges that could not have been prevented. Again, we cannot know how many more offenses they committed, nor is there any way of estimating the percentage of all the 2,892 crimes for which our 342 adult offenders and 126 juveniles were responsible. *What stands out at this point is that of the 468 adults and juveniles charged with violent crimes, 342, or 73.1 percent, could not have been prevented from committing their offenses by an incapacitating sentence under the provisions of Policy 4.*

Illuminating the Dark Side of the Data

Many readers of our reports on this experiment have seized on the virtual certainty that the incapacitation of the recidivists for the five-year term would have prevented a much larger fraction of the 2,892 violent crimes reported. It was pointed out that most muggers commit more muggings than those for which they are arrested. Likewise, rapists, but probably not murderers. As for aggravated assault, the reluctance of many victims to proceed with prosecution or even to cooperate with the police in clearing a report might account for many uncleared crimes.

We agreed. The difficulty with further analysis based on our data was obvious. There were 2,100 reported crimes that were not cleared by the police. If we assumed that all these reports represented the commission of real index violent offenses, was there a way to determine how many of them were preventable if our Policy 4 had been in force (that is, if all those hwo had been convicted of a felony between the years 1968 and 1973 had been incarcerated)? No exact answer to this question was possible, but on reflection we saw that ranges could be established within which the true answer must lie. The logic of our reasoning was long and complex, and I will not attempt to reproduce it in full.[5]

The beginning is the classification of the possible offenders by their status as felons with prior convictions and by their status as to actual arrests for violent crime in 1973. That resulted in a two-by-two table consisting of four quadrants, which I present here as table 5–6. This table calls for an explanation. In quadrant I are those 96 offenders whose crimes were preventable under Policy 4 because

Table 5–6
Offenders 1968 to 1973

	Felony Conviction	*No Felony Conviction*
	Quadrant I	Quadrant II
Violent Arrest in 1973	Total offenders: 96 Total offenses: 210 Murder/manslaughter: 22 Violent sex crimes: 41 Aggravated assault: 17 Robbery: 130	Total offenders: 372 Total offenses: 582 Murder/manslaughter: 42 Violent sex crimes: 120 Aggravated assault: 115 Robbery: 305
	Quadrant III	Quadrant IV
No Violent Arrest in 1973		

they had been convicted of a felony in the period 1968 to 1973. We know that they committed 210 crimes, distributed as shown. Similarly, in quadrant II we know that there were 372 offenders, adult and juvenile, with no felony convictions between 1968 and 1973. There were 582 violent felonies charged against them in 1973. Quadrants I and II rest on firmly verifiable knowledge.

With quadrants III and IV we enter a realm of speculation. There were 2100 violent crimes reported to the police in 1973 which were not cleared. They were distributed as follows:

Murder/manslaughter	1
Violent sex crimes	165
Aggravated assault	815
Robbery	1,119
Total	2,100

Those offenses that could be assigned to quadrants I or III were preventable. Those that were assigned to quadrants II or IV were not preventable. If recidivist felons had committed all the uncleared crimes, the result would be as shown in table 5–7. In this table, we assumed for the moment that all the uncleared crimes were committed by persons who would have been serving five-year terms under the provisions of Policy 4. For convenience I have assigned the uncleared crimes to quadrant III, although we can be sure that a good many of them must have been committed by the 96 individuals in quadrant I. If table 5–7 were to be believed, 70.4 percent of

Table 5–7
Maximum Prevention of 2,892 Violent Crimes, Assuming Recidivists Committed All Uncleared Crimes, 1968 to 1973

	Felony Conviction	*No Felony Conviction*
	Quadrant I	**Quadrant II**
Violent Arrest in 1973	Total offenders: 96 Total offenses: 210 Murder/manslaughter: 22 Violent sex crimes: 41 Aggravated assault: 17 Robbery: 130	Total offenders: 372 Total offenses: 582 Murder/manslaughter: 42 Violent sex crimes: 120 Aggravated assault: 115 Robbery: 305
	Quadrant III	**Quadrant IV**
No Violent Arrest in 1973	Total offenders: Unknown Total offenses: 2100 Murder/manslaughter: 1 Violent sex crimes: 165 Aggravated assault: 815 Robbery: 1,119	Total offenders: Unknown Total offenses: Assume none

the violent crimes committed in Columbus in 1973 could have been prevented by the application of Policy 4.

But table 5–7 makes no sense at all. It stands to reason that the "virgins" in quadrant II must have committed some uncleared crimes. As persons previously unknown to the police, it would be probable that they could have been responsible for a very substantial share. Further, there must have been some crimes committed by itinerant criminals passing through Columbus and some that were committed by "virgins" who were never arrested for anything and got off scot-free. They belong in quadrant IV.

We proceeded to distribute the uncleared crimes by offense category to the four quadrants. That process imposed some ceilings on quadrants I and II. For example, there were 26 sex offenders in quadrant I. We supposed that each of them might have committed an additional offense with which he was not charged. There were 86 sex offenders in quadrant II about whom we made the same assumption. Obviously, some probably committed more than one uncleared offense. That meant that others committed only the offenses for which they were arrested. This division left 53 sex offenses to divide between quadrants III and IV. At that point we had to be arbitrary. We decided that 28 belonged in quadrant III and 25 in quadrant IV.

We went through the same exercise with the aggravated assaults and the robbers. We assigned four uncleared assaults to the assaultists in quadrants I and II and three uncleared robberies to each of the known robbers. The one uncleared homicide was arbitrarily assigned to quadrant III, with full recognition that it might have been appropriately assigned to any of the other three.

Table 5–8 shows our best estimate of the distribution of the offenses among the four quadrants. While there may be differences of opinion about the estimates we have made, the range of preventable crimes narrowly limits the speculations. Table 5–8 allows a level of prevention of 34.4 percent. The not unreasonable assumption that the uncleared crimes not assigned to quadrants I and II could be distributed in the same proportions to quadrants III and IV results in a level of percentage of 25.0 percent. Assigning all the uncleared crimes to quadrant III, an unreasonable assumption, results in a preventable percentage of 47.6 percent. We think that it is most likely that the proportion of preventable crime in this study is roughly one-third.

But this exercise has assumed all along the impossible Policy 4,

Table 5–8
Maximum Distribution of 2,892 Violent Crimes under Policy 4, 1968 to 1973

	Felony Conviction	*No Felony Conviction*
	Quadrant I	**Quadrant II**
Violent Arrest in 1973	Total offenders: 96 Total offenses: 563 Murder/manslaughter: 23 Violent sex crimes: 67 Aggravated assault: 73 Robbery: 400 Total: 563	Total offenders: 372 Total offenses: 1,516 Murder/manslaughter: 42 Violent sex crimes: 206 Aggravated assault: 459 Robbery: 809
	Quadrant III	**Quadrant IV**
No Violent Arrest in 1973	Total offenders: unknown Total offenses: 431 Murder/manslaughter: 1 Violent sex crimes: 28 Aggravated assault: 220 Robbery: 182	Total offenders: unknown Total offenses: 382 Murder/manslaughter: 0 Violent sex crimes: 25 Aggravated assault: 195 Robbery: 162

the economic and social cost of which would be enormous—as I will show in the concluding section of this chapter. We made some additional calculations for Policies 5 and 10. The strict application of Policy 5 (which called for a five-year sentence for a second felony conviction for either juveniles or adults) would have prevented about 17 percent of the 1973 violent crimes. It is doubtful that this severe statute could be enacted. In applying Policy 10 (five years flat for any *violent* felony, a sanction that might well be enacted throughout the country), we found that 9.8 percent of the violent crimes would have been prevented. The prevention of 10 percent of the violence in Columbus is an objective worth a considerable cost, but it must not be assumed that a penal statute of this kind will greatly increase the safety of the citizens.

A Rough Estimate of the False-Positives

It is one thing to sentence an offender for a specific crime to a specific term in prison. The penalty may be too heavy or too light, but it will be based exclusively on a verdict of guilty. It is quite another thing to sentence an offender according to an expectation of what he will do if left at large, as would be the case if our Policy 4 were to be unflinchingly applied. In this case, the statute would be in force because of a prediction that any person convicted of any felony will have a high probability of committing a major violent crime. If this prediction is generally correct, perhaps at the level of nine out of ten cases, a good deal of support might be mobilized for such a statute, in spite of the huge expense. But to the extent that the prediction turns out to be wrong rather than right, this policy will be an instrument of injustice.

We had no direct method of determining the number of false-positives for our study cohort. Recognizing the importance of the problem, we created a study group consisting of all the persons arrested for violent crimes during the year 1966. There were 164 whose criminal careers we could trace.

Of the 164 persons arrested, 103 were eventually convicted. Ten were convicted of nonviolent offenses, and we did not trace their subsequent careers. Five were incarcerated for more than five years, and we dropped them out of consideration. Of the remaining 88, some did some time, others were placed on probation. All were in the community for most of the five years after their conviction. A total of 18 were rearrested during this period on charges of violent offenses, 9 were convicted—10.2 percent of those released.

This study would be a test of our Policy 10 (five years for the conviction of any violent felony). It leads to an extremely small number of true-positives. Policy 4 would surely produce a great many more false-positives and even fewer true-positives.

The Heavy Cost of the Hard Line

A penal policy that would lead to so much injustice must be unacceptable in a society committed to fairness for all citizens. But in
addition to the unfair incapacitation of large numbers of criminals,
the unavoidable economic costs would be intolerable. To calculate
the fiscal consequences, we engaged in some simple but impressive
arithmetic.

In 1972 there were 1,091 adult felony convictions in Franklin
County, resulting in 438 prison sentences. We assumed that those
who were committed to prison averaged a two-year term. Then we
supposed that all the 1,091 persons convicted received five-year sentences without remission. The result was a total of 4,629 additional
man-years of incarceration from Franklin County alone.[6] If Franklin
County felons accumulated at the same rate for five years, the additional burden on the overpopulated Ohio prisons would be 4,600.
Perhaps that figure is too high. We reduced it by 40 percent, arriving
at an additional commitment of 2,760 prisoners from Franklin County
alone. The population of Franklin County is about one-twelfth that
of Ohio. Policy 4 would therefore increase the population of Ohio
prisons (whose normal capacity was about 9,000) by about 33,000.

These figures were calculated from a 1972 base. During the remaining years of the 1970s the volume of crime increased substantially in Ohio, as elsewhere throughout the nation. The 33,000
additional prisoners would be far less than the magnitude of the
increase that would have been required ten years later. We did not
attempt to calculate the costs of construction and maintenance of
the additional prisons that would be required by Policy 4. Like many
other large states, Ohio has had to engage in a major prison construction program to accommodate a population approaching 20,000
prisoners in 1984. The large sums of money for capital costs and
annual maintenance for the years ahead would be much more than
doubled if Policy 4 were adopted.

Replication of any experiment is a welcome confirmation of findings. Using a methodology similar to ours, Petersilia and Greenwood
calculated the impact of our Policy 4 on urban violence in Denver.
They found that its adoption in that city during the years 1968 to
1970 would have resulted in an increase in the Colorado prison
population on the order of 450 percent. The reduction in the number
of violent crimes would have been about 31 percent. In addition,
they calculated the value of a one-year sentence for any felony and

found that the reduction of violent crimes would be about 10.9 percent with an increase in prison population of about 25 percent.[7]

Have we demolished a straw man? Many readers must be inclined to challenge the usefulness of this research. No state legislature would be likely to enact the incapacitating statutes that our hypothetical policies would call for. Why go to all this trouble to prove that the impractical is also ineffective?

The answer must be sought in the temper of the times. The American people have learned that prisons cannot be hospitals dedicated to the cure of criminality. Some criminals complete their terms the better for their chastening experience, but not by prescription. Others are so frightened by the hazards of daily life in prison as to be effectively intimidated. But neither rehabilitation nor intimidation is reliably working to reduce the volume of crime. It is widely supposed that if prisons can neither cure criminals nor scare them straight, at least they can contain them. This study shows that even with an extravagant policy of incapacitation the reduction in the volume of crime will not be equally impressive. Other answers are possible, and they must be sought.

Notes

1. James Q. Wilson, *Thinking About Crime* (New York: Basic Books, 1975).

2. *Ibid.*, 209. In the revised edition of this book, Wilson deleted his generalization about the likes and inclinations of intellectuals, limiting himself to the unarguable statement that "wicked people exist." *Thinking About Crime*, rev. ed. (New York: Basic Books, 1983), 260.

3. Stephan Van Dine, John P. Conrad, and Simon Dinitz, *Restraining the Wicked* (Lexington, Mass.: Lexington Books, 1979). See pp. 54–56 for an account of the criteria for each of the 16 policies tested. The effectiveness of each policy is shown in table 4–11 on p. 98.

4. *Ibid.*, 64–81.

5. *Ibid.*, 116–22.

6. *Ibid.*, 123–24.

7. Joan Petersilia and Peter W. Greenwood, *Mandatory Prison Sentences: Their Projected Effects on Crime and Prison Population* (Santa Monica: Rand Corporation, 1977).

6
The Utilitarian Delusion

Jeremy Bentham's Legacy

The English-speaking world is burdened with Benthamite thought about the administration of justice. Whatever the merits of utilitarian public philosophy may be for guidance in other domains of government, it has raised grossly unrealistic expectations of the criminal law, sentencing, and penology. To Bentham and his disciples it was clear that if justice is efficiently administered, crime can be controlled, if not eliminated. Consider Bentham's basic theorem on punishment:

> [A]ll punishment is mischief: all punishment in itself is evil. Upon the principle of utility, if it ought at all to be admitted, it ought only to be admitted in as far as it promises to exclude some greater evil. . . . The immediate principal end of punishment is to control action. This action is either that of the offender, or of others: that of the offender it controls by its influence, either on his will, in which case it is said to operate in the way of *reformation*, or on his physical power, in which case it is said to operate by *disablement*: that of others it can influence no otherwise than by its influence over their wills, in which case it is said to operate in the way of *example*.[1]

The trinity of utilitarian objectives has survived in the pieties of abstract criminological discourse, if less evident in the practical administration of justice. We choose a different vocabulary, preferring *rehabilitation, incapacitation,* and *general deterrence.* In Bentham's time, the utilitarian commitment to the prevention of crime was a vast advance over eighteenth-century retributivism. The predilection of English justice for hanging criminals was matched by even more barbarous punishment on the Continent. While savage retributive justice was certainly intended to have the secondary effects of "disablement" and "example," the dominant legislative motive was to destroy the criminal as society's enemy.[2] Influenced by Beccaria,[3] Jeremy Bentham offered his contemporaries an approach to punishment that broke with the tradition of ferocious retributivism. To prevent crime, there are principles that make better sense than the gallows or the guillotine.

During the century and a half that followed the passing of the industrious Bentham, generations of penologists adopted his plausible utilitarianism, whether they had ever heard of Bentham—let alone ploughed through his indigestible prose—or not. The immediate benefits of penological Benthamism cannot be denied. He was one of the principal actors in a revolution in criminal justice, a revolution that civilized a process that degraded all its participants.

His doctrines were formulated with some attention to principle and were accompanied by specific instructions as to their most effective application. He was a social engineer, perhaps the first in modern history, as well as a social architect. He left his blueprints behind, though few of them materialized in actual structures.

Many of his attempts to increase the happiness of all by redesigning society now seem absurd. For penologists, the Panopticon, the stillborn innovation with which he expected to solve the problem of crime and perhaps all other social problems, is a typically naive example of Benthamite social architecture. Even more outlandish was his confidence that he could enrich himself by managing England's prisons as a private enterprise. Nevertheless, he deserves credit as the first planner of social change.[4] His designs have been reduced to dusty curiosa, but his ideas have been durable influences on thought about punishment.

Under Bentham's surviving but now almost invisible sway, most penologists and most of the public to this day suppose that the proper mission of criminal justice is the reduction of crime. It follows that the system succeeds to the extent that the crime rate falls, and fails when it rises. If that is a reasonable basis for evaluation, U.S. criminal justice has been a resounding failure for most of the four decades since the end of World War II.

That pronouncement has been loudly and frequently made. Critics of criminal justice from both the left and the right have accepted that reasoning and concluded that the failure is irrefutable evidence that something is wrong, disastrously wrong. Far out on the left, the word is that prisons must be abolished or, at most, that only the really dangerous offenders should be caged in them—and those for as short a time as possible.[5] If notice is taken of Benthamism, such critics will urge its discard. The late French philosopher and social historian Michel Foucault correctly noted that Benthamism, as mediated through the famous Panopticon or by any other penal facility, becomes an instrument of the state's absolute power over the individual—power that, it is to be inferred from his argument, no state should have.[6]

On the right end of the discourse, the inference to be drawn from the failure of criminal justice to achieve the Benthamite goals is implacable. For the hard-line critic, the system is a perversion of Benthamism. Instead of Bentham's "hedonic calculus"—the calibration of punishment at a higher cost than the gain from the criminal act—liberal judges and legislators have reduced sanctions to a meaningless leniency. The death penalty has been all but abolished. Sentences are so mild as to be meaningless. The answer? Longer terms of incarceration for all felony offenses, the return of the death penalty for homicide, and strict limits on the appellate process.[7]

Both positions are built on the supposed failure of criminal justice to achieve the three Benthamite objectives. That both positions are about equally unrealistic troubles their exponents not at all. If, as some radical reformers urge, a general amnesty is declared for most, if not all prisoners, and imprisonment comes to an end, another solution to the crime problem will emerge—from what source other than the presumed altruism of the generous American public we are never informed.

The advocates of increased severity know that their solution will be costly in the short run and that the costs will be paid in crowded and dangerous prisons and the construction of expensive new facilities. In the long run, so the neoconservative reformer holds (though the name of Bentham is seldom invoked nor is his terminology put on display), a return to Bentham's hedonic calculus through the legislation and imposition of realistically long sentences will eventually reduce the volume of crime to such an extent that the short-term outlay will be an investment richly rewarded by a great reduction in crime.

I have devoted this attention to the present status of Benthamism because in this chapter I want to consider the implications of Dangerous Offender research for the cardinal utilitarian objectives of deterrence, rehabilitation, and incapacitation. The great attraction of these two objectives is that they *are* objectives. American culture prods both individuals and institutions to order their existence toward the achievement of goals. For criminal justice, the reduction of crime is the goal to be achieved, and the means toward that end is the greatest possible accomplishment of the grand utilitarian objectives.

Moreover, measurement of achievement should settle the value of the institutions of justice and the competence of those who administer them. To restrain a recidivist by locking him up should prevent all the crimes that might be committed by that particular criminal. If all the crimes that each restrained recidivist might have committed could be summed into a total and applied to the crime rate, it should follow that the crime rate would eventually show a substantial decline. Further benefits of extended restraint would accure from the intimidation of the confined recidivist and the example of his fate as conveyed to the potential criminal. The degree to which these benefits are achieved should be at least roughly measurable, and thereby the "success" or "failure" of criminal justice could be gauged.

Our data lead us in another direction. To look for the success or failure of criminal justice in the achievement or nonachievement of these goals is a futile pursuit of a will-o'-the-wisp. Modern criminologists, with access to statistical methods of extraordinary abstruseness and the computers to apply them, will continue the search for ever more sensitive indices of goal achievement. But legislators and judges enact and enforce laws that are intended to give the criminal his due. Punishment is gauged on a retributivist scale, inevitably shifting with the sense of public opinion and, it must be recognized, sometimes with judicial idiosyncrasy. If utilitarian goals are achieved, they are secondary to meting out to the criminal his just desert. The success of criminal justice must be measured in intangibles: a sense of fairness, efficiency in administration, and integrity in management. None of these qualities lends itself to statistical evaluation.

Example and Deterrence

Concerning the grand objective of general deterrence, the Dangerous Offender Project must be silent. Nothing in our data entitles us to make statements about the effectiveness of general deterrence of violent offenses in Columbus. I doubt that anyone is in possession of empirical support for the expectation that the penalty structure of the criminal law or the enforcement activities of the system succeed or fail to deter crime. The scientific situation has been well and tersely stated by Zimring:

> Unless one accepts the analogies of positive economics or the easy insights of armchair theory, our present knowledge of deterrence is singularly bereft of a general theoretical structure with which to incorporate and organize particular experimental findings. While the range of analogies to problems of deterrence is both wide and

inviting, the number of established crime-specific theoretical propositions is discouragingly small.[8]

Although the empirical criminologist must withhold comment on the effectiveness of general deterrence in limiting crime, much more can and should be said about "specific" deterrence or, to put the matter bluntly, the intimidation of the offender. In chapter 4 we saw that although a substantial number of first offenders in our study of the careers of violent offenders seemed to vanish from the data, the real careerists, the chronic recidivists, continued in criminal activity through many arrests, almost as many convictions, and frequent prison sentences. All these transactions between system and offender are matters of record, usually representing offenses of some moment, sufficient to submit to the Federal Bureau of Investigation for inclusion in the individual's "rap-sheet" or criminal history. No one can say for sure how many unreported or uncleared offenses these men committed, but there can be no doubt that there were more, probably many more.

This aspect of sentencing has not been a subject of systematic research. In its recent review, the National Research Council's Panel on Sentencing Research is silent on the differential outcomes of sentences by length, severity, and type as applied to different classes of offender. We cannot turn to an established body of research that will inform the policy-maker regarding experience with penalties in intimidating specific classes of offenders.[9]

The obstacles to research of this kind are many but not insuperable. It is often argued that the effects of rehabilitative processes cannot be reliably separated from the intimidating effect of punishment. As Nigel Walker remarks, "such evidence as there is suggests very strongly that both processes take place."[10] I accept that strong suggestion, and I cannot see that it should prevent the systematic study of the complex rehabilitation/intimidation variable. I suspect that in most situations intimidation has more to do with the desired change than group counseling or vocational training—but I would be pleased if my suspicion were to be proved wrong.

More serious is the observable fact that although for some punishment is effectively intimidating, for others the available punishments are acceptable, if not even attractive. Our findings in chapters 3 and 4, showing that some first offenders disappear from the annals of crime whereas others go on to long, undeterred, and evidently satisfying criminal careers could be duplicated in the data banks of any state correctional system. It would be worth a great deal to know the differences between the first-term convicts who disappear from the FBI files and those other first-termers who spend their manhood alternating between the streets and the prison yard. Unfortunately, our study was not equipped to make this discrimination.

The state of research on individual deterrence, or intimidation, allows the formulation of no principle. The exhaustive study of deterrence by Zimring and Hawkins winds down to many questions and no answers:

> In the light of the paucity of available evidence it is difficult to offer firm conclusions regarding the way in which punishment will affect punished offenders' responses to legal threats. . . . [I]n respect both to the timing of punishment and to the details of it, it seems plausible to assume that experience of punishment will condition future threat responsiveness. . . . [I]n neither case will it necessarily be in the direction of increased sensitivity to threats.[11]

The evidence presented in chapter 4 amply confirms the ambivalent conclusion of these authors. The diminished sensitivity of the Columbus recidivist calls for an intensive study of alternative controls. It does not indicate that more recidivists should be locked up for longer periods.

Does Anything Work?

If there is any staple of the criminological literature that is universally known among penologists it is the late Robert Martinson's review of the evaluations of rehabilitation programs for offenders.[12] Although his article does not contain the phrase, its import can be encapsulated in two words: *Nothing works.* Pessimism has never been more parsimoniously expressed or more widely influential. In more ample terms, his conclusion was, "With few and isolated exceptions, the rehabilitative efforts that have been reported so far have had no appreciable effect on recidivism." So much for Bentham's declaration that the aim of punishment should be the reformation of the offender.

Elsewhere I have dealt with the "rehabilitative ideal" to which Martinson was thought to have administered a *coup de grace*.[13] As an ideal it commanded much lip-service but no serious striving. Even where there were fairly determined efforts to rehabilitate offenders, as there were in California for the twenty years preceding the mid-1960s, sentencing decisions were made on a clearly retributive consideration of the adequacy of the punishment, not by the light of a utilitarian ideal.

The notion that the indeterminate sentence made possible a sentencing decision that tied the release of the convict to his progress toward a Benthamite "reformation" was bogus from the first. The community nuisance, a joy-riding young auto thief, a check-writer, a petty grifter would hardly ever make any such progress, but regardless of his prospects for a reformed way of life would be turned loose as soon as his minimum sentence was out of the way. Public funds were not to be wasted on attempts to achieve the obviously impossible. A penitent murderer or rapist, eager to reform and making discernible progress toward the goal of social restoration would nevertheless have to serve all the years that were appropriate for the gravity of his crime.

The indeterminate sentence, as it has been administered everywhere that I have seen, serves two very practical purposes, neither of which has anything to do with the *"rehabilitative* ideal." First, it is a useful device for equalizing sentences. Where scores, sometimes hundreds of judges and juries are participating in the sentencing process, a paroling authority will assure that judges posturing for a hard-line community cannot impose outlandish sentences merely to please their neighbors and constituents.[14] Parole boards are open to many severe criticisms, many of which I have made as vigorously as I could, but their position as the final arbiter of the time to be served makes equity possible—though not inevitable.

The second use of the indeterminate sentence is to maintain prison discipline. As an incentive to comply with the rules, none of the procedures in the repertory of a prison warden compares to his influence on the time a convict—or a "student" in a "training school"—must serve until he is released. When a disciplinary infraction can be punished, not only with immediate consequences (such as consignment to a segregated cell-block or solitary confinement) but also with a deferred release date, the number of potential rule infractors can be reduced to the relatively few incorrigibles who have nothing to lose by the consequences of their behavior. Few parole boards will agree to the release of chronic rule violators without some evidence that a mending of errant ways has taken place.

Both of these purposes are legitimate and necessary, but neither has anything at all to do with rehabilitation in the sense of substantial attitude and behavior change. It is beside the point that I want to make here that there are other and more equitable means to both these ends. For the equalization of sentences, the establishment of a Sentencing Review Commission, charged with the administration of a system of guidelines would allay that vexation. For the maintenance of discipline, a honestly managed system of "good time" for the remission of sentences and the award of privileges for unblemished behavior is much more equitable than a parole board could possibly be.

What neither the public nor many veteran functionaries of criminal justice nor most academic criminologists have understood is the circular reasoning that has supported a belief in the primacy of rehabilitation as a purpose of punishment. The requirement that criminal offenders should change their ways is considered self-evident. No offender should be released until rehabilitated. Therefore the indeterminate sentence. The existence of the indeterminate sentence demonstrates the intent to rehabilitate. Therefore it follows that rehabilitation is the objective of punitive sentencing. The insistent emphasis on the importance of rehabilitation by U.S. and British penologists adds powerful support to their fragile logic. To hold aloft the rehabilitative ideal as the mission of penology is to polish their vocation with a glow of altruism.

Wholly apart from the bedraggled evaluations on which Martinson based his conclusions, it should always have been evident that rehabilitative programs did not and could not work as effective measures to reform offenders, and for two reasons. First, it is rare indeed that any program could be prescribed that would offset the condition of the offender in the community, confronted with ostracism, an impoverished environment, criminal peers and acquaintances, and the antisocial habits of a lifetime. Second, it has never been possible to administer an incarcerative facility as a benign agency of rehabilitation. The primary objective of the administration of such a facility must be the maintenance of effective control. Control requires the firm coercion of all persons within the facility, staff and prisoners alike. It depends on manifest disincentives. There are few carrots, but the sticks are heavy.[15]

Most contemporary penologists understand that coerced rehabilitation was never the ideal that their naive predecessors supposed. They generally subscribe to the valid notion that self-improvement is the affair of the person to be improved. The state's interest is served by making available the means toward that end, recognizing that the convict in prison can choose for himself only what the prison authorities can offer. In that way, the rehabilitative program is no longer a distant ideal to be held out to all, but a practical hope for each individual still capable of hoping for a constructive life. Rehabilitative programs can and do work when they are offered, not prescribed. Their effectiveness in reducing recidivism should not be the measure that validates their usefulness. As with any activity intended for anyone's self-improvement, their measure of effectiveness should be successful completion. In prison the justification of their presence is the hope that dies with their absence. There are many more reasons for the recidivism of an offender than the insufficiency of his efforts to make something better for himself.

Jeremy Bentham's concept of reformation depended on the power of the state. Whatever the resident of his Panopticon did was to be in response to the requirement of an all-seeing monitor stationed in the tower at the center of the rotunda. That monitor never materialized in the modern prison. In his stead, there are counselors, guards and classification committees, all supposed to combine in the exercise of that absolute control. Control of the hours, the comings and goings, the food and the work is always feasible, and prison staff have become good at maintaining that kind of control of the externalities of incarcerated life. Control of attitudes and beliefs is even more difficult in prison than it is outside. It doesn't work, it has never worked, and it never will.

The utilitarian ideal of reformation was always a delusion. The absurdities of program evaluation by the gauge of recidivism can be put behind us, as silly statistical exercises into which too much energy and talent have been diverted. Reality requires an appreciation of the complexity of change. Delusions escape reality in search of the comfort of simplicities.

Selection for Disablement

Chapter 5 reported our experiment with incapacitation and concluded that although the amount of violent crime could be reduced by locking up specified felons for long periods of time after their conviction, this result could be achieved only at the cost of a large increase in the number of criminals convicted and also with a substantial number of them being needlessly confined. As a policy for crime reduction, both the moral and the economic costs were excessive.

Our experiment was crude. We did not discriminate the felons to be restrained by their commitment to criminality. We prescribed their incarceration if they met certain criteria: a felony conviction within the last three or five years, or convictions of violent crimes within some period of time. We could estimate the number of uncleared crimes that would be prevented by incarcerating *all* the persons who had committed felonies or certain types of felonies within some period of time. We could not pick and choose offenders according to their personal records of uncleared crimes.

In their report, *Selective Incapacitation,* Greenwood and Abrahamse hurdled this methodological obstacle.[16] His colleagues had engaged in a reconnaissance of self-reported criminal histories at a California prison.[17] Noticing that these histories varied greatly in the numbers of uncleared crimes reported, these researchers decided that incapacitation might be a successful strategy for crime control if those offenders could be selected who were most likely to commit the most crimes. The reconnaissance was followed by a survey of 2,190 prisoners in California, Texas, and Michigan intended to explore further the differences in the "rates" of offending among confined prisoners. It was discovered that the reconnaissance had been correct. The prisoners varied from men who had reported no uncleared crimes, to men who claimed over 200 burglaries in a year. The respondents could be trichotomized into three classes: low-rate, medium-rate, and high-rate offenders. The low-rate offenders committed crimes at a frequency below the median. The medium-rate offenders operated between the 50th and the 75th percentiles. The high-rate offenders, the focus of Greenwood's attention, occupy the right-hand tail of the distribution and committed crimes at frequencies above the 75th percentile. With the personal histories of the respondents in hand, Greenwood's next task was to discover a way to identify those whose rates of criminal activity fell into each of these categories. The result was a system of prediction that depended on the addition of seven binary variables:

1. Prior conviction for the instant offense type
2. Incarcerated more than 50 percent of the preceding two years
3. Conviction before age 16
4. Served time in a state juvenile facility
5. Drug use in preceding two years
6. Drug use as a juvenile
7. Employed less than 50 percent of the preceding two years

Scoring 1 for a yes and 0 for a no, the offender's predicted rate of criminality could be obtained. A score of 0 to 1 was a low-rate offender, a score of 2 to 3 was medium-rate, and 4 to 7 identified the high-rate offenders. Applying this system to a sample of 781 burglars and robbers, Greenwood obtained the distribution found in table 6–1.

It will be seen from table 6–1 that Greenwood's false-positives add up to 26 percent of his sample. The false-negatives are 23 percent. Of the 29 percent of the sample identified as high-rate offenders, only 51.7 percent are correctly identified. The remainder consists of medium- and low-rate offenders. If a rationale could be conceived that would justify the restraint of so large a proportion of false-

Table 6–1
Predicted versus Self-Reported Offense Rates for Robbery and Burglary
(in percentage, N = 781)

Score on Predic-	Self-Reported Offense Rates			
tion Scale	*Low*	*Medium*	*High*	*Total*
Low (0–1)	14	10	3	27
Medium (2–3)	12	22	10	44
High (4–7)	4	10	15	29
Total	30	42	28	100

Note: Each respondent is compared only against other respondents from his state who were convicted of the same offense type.

positives, the way was clear, in Greenwood's opinion, to reduce crime while at the same time keeping prison populations within present bounds.

It would be a pointless digression to rehearse all Greenwood's hypothetical sentencing policies here. The reader may review them in his monograph. Their general drift may be surmised from Greenwood's estimate that if only high-rate offenders are sentenced to prison (the others receiving short jail sentences or going on probation), the California prison population would be kept at 95 percent of capacity while reducing the volume of crime by 15 percent. The medium- and low-rate offenders would be sentenced to jail or placed on probation, thereby reserving costly prison space for those from whom the public needed the most protection. The lesson that medium- and low-rate hoodlums would draw from their selection for leniency is left to speculation. I would suppose that some might conclude that the trade-off of jail for an occasional robbery or burglary is not an unsatisfactory transaction.

As a concept and as a product of the basic research on habitual offenders, *Selective Incapacitation* has been widely criticized.[19] Although Greenwood has made presentations to sympathetic audiences of prosecutors, legislators, and police officials, his fellow criminologists have not been nearly so approving. Their criticisms have been advanced on both moral and empirical grounds. Because the issues raised by selective incapacitation are fundamental to the application of research to policy, I want to review both sides in this probably irreconcilable conflict.[20]

Reliance on Self-Reports

Greenwood conceded that the basis of his system consists of self-reports of juvenile records, drug use, and employment. He agreed that this data base could be improved, perhaps with drug testing at the time of arrest.

Jan and Marcia Chaiken, who conducted the original survey, made a careful analysis of the problem of its reliability and validity. Like Greenwood, they were senior members of the Rand research staff. They had worked with the same questionnaires and had conscientiously tried to assess their validity, even though they did not consider that their findings justified a model for decision-making in sentencing. Their conclusions were cautious and too detailed to reproduce here. However, they decided that after the completion of numerous checks with official records and for internal consistency of the responses, they could trust the veracity of about 83 percent of the respondents.[21]

Marquis and Ebener, also of Rand, had previously studied the reliability of self-report questionnaires in exhaustive detail. They found that arrests and convictions were reported without bias in the direction of over- and underreporting, but with "moderate to large amounts of random errors that will yield attenuated estimates of the true population associations." They did not attempt to assess the veracity of self-reports of *uncleared* crimes committed. It is probable that the random errors in reports of events that were on official record would be even more frequent as to events that were recorded only in the uncertain memories of even the most honest and painstaking criminal respondents.[22]

That point deserves some emphasis. I do not take issue with the concept of the self-report as a vehicle for getting information on personal behavior that is available by no other method. As an instrument of reconnaissance, it will often be an indispensable aid to social research as in the Chaikens' survey. However, to expect accurate and dependable recall from the confused, poorly lettered, and poorly ordered minds of a population of criminal offenders—even for a brief and relatively recent "window period"—is an act of faith on which no enduring structure for decision-making should be built. To suppose that such a survey could support a sentencing model on which decisions about long-term incarceration would be made is to introduce scientism as a substitute for intuition and judgment in decision-making.

The Restricted Sample

The samples on which Greenwood relied consisted of prisoners from certain facilities in California, Michigan, and Texas. The assumption is implicit that a universe of offenders has been surveyed in California, and likewise in Michigan and Texas. Although jail prisoners were also included in the study, there was no attempt to encompass a more comprehensive universe. No probationers, no arrestees awaiting trial—the latter an improbable group of potential respondents. Greenwood dismissed in advance what would have been a captious objection that no uncaught offenders were included. However, attempts should have been made to obtain self-reports from probationers to determine the extent to which their criminal experience might have altered the base of the model. This is a technical fault that can be readily corrected in a future study. If the Greenwood scale is taken as a pilot test of a method, that objection need not be taken very seriously.

The False-Positive, False-Negative Problem

The usefulness of any model of incapacitation depends from first to last on the false-positive problem, to which I have given much attention in earlier chapters. In acting against an offender on a prediction that he is *probably* going to commit a crime unless he is restrained, the system of criminal justice is doing exactly what some judges and prosecutors, and most forensic psychiatrists, parole boards, and other decision-makers and influencers have been doing for generations.

To sentence a convicted criminal on a probability has no sanction in legal theory, but plenty of support in utilitarian doctrine. It is fair to say that not many of those who must make decisions on such a foundation would care to put a numerical value on the probability of recidivism, but many of them would claim some approach to certainty. Any supporter of the retributivist doctrine of "just deserts" will reject such claims and the resort to probabilistic sentencing for the purpose of incapacitation.

It can never be certain how many false-positives are contained among Greenwood's high-rate offenders, but estimates vary from 4 percent to about 57 percent. Greenwood thinks that about 4 percent of his high-rate offenders are actually low-raters, a lenient view of the matter. A recalculation by Jacqueline Cohen of the Carnegie-Mellon University shows that of the high-rate offenders 56.6 percent were either medium- or low-rate.[23] I have noted before (p. 101) that of those predicted to be high-rate offenders 48.3 percent were either medium- or low-rate. Whatever the true figure must be, a scale that predicts with a margin of error hovering around 50 percent does not select reliably enough to justify incapacitation, even by the loosest utilitarian criteria.

I will not address the false-negative problem in detail. Nevertheless, a system that will predict success and produce failure in substantial amounts will not contribute to the public's confidence in criminal justice. The Greenwood scale will generate almost as many false-negatives as it will false-positives. The consequences of judicial reliance on a "scientific" scale that produces such abundant errors will be serious. What little social science can contribute to effective functioning of criminal justice will be called into question and proposed for discard in favor of a harder line than ever.

The Enhancement of Sentences

Let us suppress the empirical objections with which I have dealt in the preceding paragraphs. Let us suppose that there is no question of the validity of the Greenwood scale, and that there are absolutely no false-positive or false-negatives to be predicted. The scale is completely valid, completely reliable. Is it an acceptable method for assuring the incapacitation of offenders?

Many would say yes, of course, and in the next breath at least some would regret that such certainties are not to be expected in this imperfect world. I will uncompromisingly insist that instruments of this kind should have no place in the routine administration of justice.

For what is the assumption about the nature of the human condition that lurks within this model? I claim that human beings are more than mere aggregates of binary variables to be totted up on a computer so that the authorities can plan for the greatest happiness of the greatest number. On the contrary, human beings change, and that is and should be critical to the human condition. We change for better or for worse, for richer or for poorer, and in sickness and in health—to quote the familiar marriage vows. So it is with the comfortable middle class, and so it is and should be with the uncomfortable poor.

The assumption implicit in the Greenwood model—or any other predictive model—is that given the unchangeable characteristics of race, age, past histories of crime and drug use, the future should be entirely predictable in terms of percentages. It then follows that the man or woman identified as a high-rate offender at the time of a first offense should be locked up for as many years as we can afford prison space for him or her, thereby saving the community countless crimes that he or she would otherwise commit. The neo-Benthamite will dismiss the possibility that a good job, a good wife, or a successful drug treatment program might offset those grimly affirmative binary variables.

So, should the state ignore a high-rate offender's long past history of crime and recidivism? What can criminology do for criminal justice if it is not allowed to predict future crimes? The answer should be found in our need to understand. The same questionnaires from which Greenwood produced *Selective Incapacitation* were designed by Jan and Marcia Chaiken to develop an empirically supportable typology. An intricate analysis created a typology of criminal careers ranging from a terrifying *violent predator* (offenders who "concurrently rob, assault, and deal drugs"), down to the comparatively harmless *"low-level drug & property offenders."* The Chaikens studied the characteristics of the careers classified by their typology, the indications of change from one type of career to another, and made a few modest suggestions for identifying a criminal as to type. In spite of their confidence in the usefulness of their findings, they insist that decisions as to disposition should not be made on the basis of their typology—which, they estimate, is subject to a 30 percent margin of error.

And what good is a typology? Criminologists have created typologies for the last thirty years. Brilliant books and articles have adorned our literature proposing and validating typologies based on various organizing principles. I would be hard pressed to demonstrate their practical value, but the Chaikens' contribution may be an exception.

For example, the "violent predator" is a source of national anxiety as well as the main object of concern in this book. The Chaikens can contribute a number of useful pieces of information about him. He is young. The average age of the violent predators in the Chaiken sample was a little less than 23 at the time of their conviction. The Chaikens found almost none among older prison populations. He is a hard drug user and usually inclined to indulge in a variety of drugs in addition to the heroin to which he is addicted. Although he is often, if not usually unemployed, he has from time to time held a legitimate job. He had an extensive juvenile record and is too young to have accumulated a series of adult convictions. He has been very assaultive and has committed a variety of crimes at a very high rate. He is usually either white or Hispanic, seldom black.

With this kind of information enabling us to identify young men of this kind, we should be able to search out a few living specimens for examination in more depth, with the aim of finding out how they got that way and what it will take to keep them from continuing their destructive course. The object is prevention and control. If we can know where these young men came from, there may be ways of diverting them from violence before it is too late. Perhaps the juvenile "training schools," in which most of them have done a stretch, could devise a longer, more specialized and effective regime. Perhaps probation and parole routines could be arranged that would put them under more effective control. We don't know now, and we won't until this research is put to use by intrepid but imaginative penologists.

And likewise with other cells in the Chaikens' typological structure. Instead of an attempt to derive a predictive strategy to incapacitate a loosely defined statistical abstraction, the Chaikens' important study offers the field a basis for exploring the behavior of living, breathing criminals—an activity that has been conspicuously dormant in contemporary criminal justice.

A Note on the Future of Prediction

In his thoughtful monograph on the prediction of violence, Monahan makes two fundamental points.[24] He confirms the general opinion that accurate long-range prediction of violent behavior is not feasible. He also shows convincingly that short-range prediction may be not only feasible but a responsibility of the clinician.

In Monahan's view, statistical prediction will be useful as a means for establishing the "base rate" of "violent acts committed by other people who have been referred by the police as dangerous." Unfortunately, this rate would have to be estimated, but certainly would be different from the rate of violence in the general population. With the base rate as a statistical foundation, Monahan proposes that short-range predictions can and should be made by qualified clinicians by taking into consideration the "major situational correlates of violent behavior." Such influences as the family environment, peer environment, employment, the availability of victims, the availability of weapons, and the availability of alcohol are suggested as obvious situational predictors.

The usefulness of a predictive model such as this for a mental health clinician is obvious. With this foundation for making judgments about the immediate disposition of emergency situations, an experienced professional should be able to plan restraining interventions for brief periods of time while remedies for abnormal conditions are devised. For sentencing decisions the value of this situational prediction is not convincingly apparent. Long-range plans for the

restriction of movement and activity are virtually impossible to enforce, as probation and parole officers are well aware.

The power of successful and accurate prediction of future events
is the enviable prerogative of the natural scientist. The movement
of distant planets, the fission of an atom, the course of a disease,
and the chances of rain tomorrow are all in the predictive power of
qualified scientists. Indeed, the ability to make successful predictions is the best index of a maturing science. It is natural that social
scientists should have sought means to make predictions of equivalent accuracy. It is even more natural that this aspiration should
concentrate the attention of criminologists, who are well aware of
the potential value of a successful predictive method—if one could
ever be contrived—to the administration of justice.

The pursuit of this chimera should end. The accurate long-range
prediction of violent behavior will be forever beyond the power of
social science, just as mathematicians can never square the circle.
The belief that predictions of violent behavior, even though very
inaccurate, will serve judges and parole boards better than no predictions is wrong. Such predictions must always be intolerably inaccurate, and there is no chance that they can be improved.

Discarding the Delusion

In this chapter I have urged that the utilitarian grip on criminal
justice be loosened. To punish criminal men, women, and children
in the hope that the Benthamite goals can be accomplished and crime
can thereby be reduced is a misguided use of the state's power. It is
a delusion to suppose that crime can be controlled by measures
designed to disable or reform offenders or by the example of their
punishment to potential offenders.

In place of the utilitarian futility, I propose a return to the retributivist foundation of justice by which, I suggest, we have always
been governed. In the free countries of the West, we have shucked
off the horrors of seventeenth- and eighteenth-century retributive
justice. So long as we remain a free people we will be free of the
horrors of the Gulag Archipelago and the doctrinaire injustices of
the East. A system of punishment that relies on the imposition of
graduated social controls is all we need. Indeed, in spite of protes-
tations to the contrary, it is all we have ever had. The next step is
to apply reason and conscience to its improvement in a system of
sanctions that will administer the consequences of wrong-doing and

assure that social control is imposed fairly and appropriately on those who need it.

Notes

1. Mary Peter Mack, *A Bentham Reader*, ch. 13 of *An Introduction to the Principles of Morals and Legislation*, 1780, "Cases Unmeet for Punishment" (New York: Pegasus Press, 1969), 120.

2. Neither Parliament nor the judiciary seem to have had any compunction about the enactment and application of the death penalty for over 200 crimes, but social historians tell us that juries were frequently insubordinate to judicial instruction. In the presence of the defendant, the conviction of a crime punishable by death was often refused, in spite of conclusive evidence of guilt. See Jerome Hall, *Theft, Law, and Society* (Indianapolis: Bobbs-Merrill, 1935), 126–30. "The influence of the jury upon the transformation of the penal law was perhaps even more effective than that of the judges. By the middle of the eighteenth century the practice of returning fictitious verdicts was so widespread that it was generally recognized as a typical feature of English administration of justice." See also Leon Radzinowicz, *A History of English Criminal Law* (London: Stevens, 1948), 94–97, on the elimination of capital charges by "pious perjury" (that is, jurors violating their oaths to acquit or convict defendants on the facts presented in the trial).

3. Cesare Beccaria, *On Crimes and Punishments*, 1764, translated by Henry Paolucci (Indianapolis: Bobbs-Merrill, 1963). Beccaria's little book was well known to most educated people in the eighteenth century, but he did not base his thought on the broad foundation of utilitarianism. That feat was left to Bentham. There were rigorous lines of logic between Bentham's penal philosophy and the "greater happiness principle," from which his whole scheme of utilitarian public policy was derived. Whatever one may think about the practical effects of utilitarianism on the administration of criminal justice (and I think they have been mostly deplorable in the long range), Bentham's intellectual prowess in building his philosophical system deserves more admiration than he received from his contemporaries. It is impressive that so much attention has been given to him in recent times by philosophers of the highest eminence. See H.L.A. Hart, *Essays on Bentham* (Oxford: Clarendon Press, 1982), and Ross Harrison, *Bentham* (London: Routledge and Kegan Paul, 1983).

4. Bentham's biographers and criminological historians have been so fascinated with Bentham's ideas that his personal interests have been given little attention. While he was sure that the Panopticon would be the grand solution to the crime problem, he also expected that as the private manager of England's penal system he would be in a position to add substantially to his personal fortune. His expectations were so high that he put up thousands of pounds for the purchase of a site on which he hoped to build the first Panopticon. The British government rejected the plan, but recognized an obligation to reimburse him for the funds the he had invested. His interest

was not exclusively penological. Once the Panopticon-prison was in working order, a really grandiose project would follow: The Panopticon would be adapted to house and employ England's paupers, perhaps a million of them in 500 such facilities. Those who would privatize America's social services may adopt Bentham as their patron philosopher. Fortunately for his reputation, the common sense of the British government prevailed, and Bentham's schemes never came to anything in his own country. See Gertrude Himmelfarb, *The Idea of Poverty* (New York: Knopf, 1984), 78–85.

5. The argument for "decarceration" was well presented by Milton G. Rector in his debate with me: Milton G. Rector and John P. Conrad, *Should We Build More Prisons?* (Hackensack, N.J.: National Council on Crime and Delinquency, 1976). For a much more extreme view, see Robert Sommer, *The End of Imprisonment* (New York: The Oxford University Press, 1976). Sommer reluctantly allows that a dangerous offender might be incarcerated for six months or more, depending on a jury's judgment as to the continuing danger presented, but such detention should be reviewed every six months to be certain that the danger still existed (p. 175).

6. Michel Foucault, *Discipline and Punish: The Birth of the Prison*, translated by Alan Sheridan (New York: Vintage Books, 1979), 195–228. I will not attempt a summary of Foucault's intricate argument. It seems to me that Foucault gives Bentham the credit that is due him and eloquently describes the consequences of Benthamism that its author could not foresee—the creation of delinquent personalities and, what is at least as undesirable in Foucault's view, the "fabrication of the disciplinary individual." For a perspective on Bentham that attempts, unsuccessfully, to reduce Bentham's importance in the history of penal reform, see Michael Rustigan, "A Reinterpretation of Criminal Law Reform in Nineteenth Century England," in David Greenberg, Ed., *Crime and Capitalism* (Palo Alto: Mayfield, 1981), 255–78.

7. The consensus is not without significant differences. James Q. Wilson doubts the efficacy of capital punishment, but he is certain that Benthamite disablement can reduce crime by keeping repetitive offenders from opportunities to commit it. See his *Thinking About Crime*, 2d ed. (New York: Basic Books, 1983), 178–94. On the other hand we have Ernest van den Haag, who stoutly maintains that it is no more than good common sense to expect that murders will take place much less frequently if the executioner is employed more frequently whether they are repetitive or not. See his contributions to *The Death Penalty: A Debate* (New York: Plenum, 1983).

8. Franklin E. Zimring, "Policy Experiments in General Deterrence: 1970–1975," in Alfred Blumstein, Jacqueline Cohen, and Daniel Nagin, eds., *Deterrence and Incapacitation: Estimating the Effects of Criminal Sanctions on Crime Rates* (Washington, D.C.: National Academy of Sciences, 1978), 164. The editors of this authoritative review of theory and research are cautiously optimistic: "The current state of experimental and quasi-experimental research on deterrence . . . is discouraging. However, most of the flaws encountered are remediable through the use of more careful research designs" (p. 58). They go on to recommend a panel to search out opportunities for research arising from specific legislative changes. This

panel has not, as yet, been formed, and deterrence research continues to languish. In the meantime, Zimring's strictures on the poverty of deterrence theory continue to be as valid as ever.

9. Alfred Blumstein, Jacqueline Cohen, Susan E. Martin, and Michael H. Tonry, eds., *Research on Sentencing: The Search for Reform*, 2 vols. (Washington, D.C.: National Academy Press, 1983). This invaluable survey is limited to four topics (vol. 1, p. 7): (1) the determinants of sentencing, including discrimination and disparity; (2) the methods used to structure sentencing decisions; (3) the effects of sentencing decisions on sentencing outcomes and system operations; (4) the connections between sentencing policy and the corrections system, particularly prison populations. Nothing is said in the voluminous text concerning the connections between sentencing decision structures and recidivism.

10. Nigel Walker, *Crime and Punishment in Britain* (Edinburgh: Edinburgh University Press, 1965), 254.

11. Franklin E. Zimring and Gordon J. Hawkins, *Deterrence: The Legal Threat in Crime Control* (Chicago: University of Chicago Press, 1973), 246.

12. Robert Martinson, "What Works? Questions and Answers about Prison Reform" *Public Interest* (1935):22–54. This famous article is based on the large and chaotically organized review of a study of 231 evaluations of correctional treatment programs undertaken between 1945 and 1968, found in Douglas Lipton, Robert Martinson, and Judith Wilks, *The Effectiveness of Correctional Treatment* (New York: Praeger, 1975). The literature in support of Martinson and in opposition is summarized in Lee Sechrest, Susan O. White, and Elizabeth D. Brown, eds., *The Rehabilitation of Criminal Offenders: Problems and Prospects* (Washington, D.C.: National Academy of Sciences, 1979), 27–34.

13. John P. Conrad, "A Lost Ideal, A New Hope: The Way toward Effective Correctional Treatment," *Journal of Criminal Law and Criminology* 72 (4) (winter 1981): 1699–1734.

14. This argument has been forcefully made by Caleb Foote. See his article, "Deceptive Determinate Sentencing," in *Determinate Sentencing: Proceedings of the Special Conference on Determinate Sentencing, 2–3 June 1977* (Washington, D.C., U.S. Department of Justice, March 1978), pp. 133–41. Professor Foote insisted that it was "absolutely essential" to retain parole boards if untrammeled discretion continued to be exercised at the earlier stages of the criminal justice process. He doubted that a "guidelines" approach could be effective in correcting disparities because too many variables have to be considered, more than a judge can take into account in his consideration of an appropriate sentence. I am unconvinced by this argument. It appears to me that guidelines that establish maximums and minimums for the sentence of any offender according to the gravity of his offense and his history of recidivism should be within the competence of any judge of reasonable intelligence to administer. As the advocates of such guidelines specify, it should be possible to deviate from either the minimum or maximum for reasons that would be placed in the offender's permanent record and made available to the public. Such a system has the advantage of honest simplicity that the old-fashioned parole board was never able to achieve.

15. For a thorough exposition of the primacy of control over treatment,

see Elliot Studt, Sheldon Messinger, and Thomas P. Wilson, *C-Unit: The Search for Community in Prison* (New York: Russell Sage Foundation, 1969).

16. Peter W. Greenwood with Alan Abrahamse, *Selective Incapacitation* (Santa Monica: Rand Corporation, August 1982).

17. Joan Petersilia and Peter W. Greenwood, with Marvin Lavin, *Criminal Careers of Habitual Felons* (Santa Monica: Rand Corporation, 1977).

18. Greenwood with Abrahamse, *Selective Incapacitation*, 59, table 4-8.

19. The most thorough review of the expanding literature on *Selective Incapacitation* is contained in an essay by John Blackmore and Jane Welsh, "Selective Incapacitation: Sentencing According to Risk," in *Crime and Delinquency* 29 (4) (October 1983): 504–28. See also my critique in "News of the Future," *Federal Probation* 46 (4) (December 1982): 69–72.

20. In this discussion I am drawing on Blackmore and Welsh, "Selective Incapacitation," and on Greenwood's own anticipation of criticism, in Greenwood with Abrahamse, *Selective Incapacitation*, 92–94.

21. Jan M. Chaiken and Marcia R. Chaiken, *Varieties of Criminal Behavior* (Santa Monica: Rand Corporation, August 1982). For a detailed account of their methods in assessing the veracity of the self-report questionnaires, see their appendix B, summarized on pp. 223–26. The complete review of their quality control procedures, which I recommend to anyone intending to conduct a similar survey, extends to p. 251. See also a condensed "executive summary," published separately, Jan M. Chaiken and Marcia R. Chaiken with Joyce E. Peterson, *Varieties of Criminal Behavior, Summary and Policy Implications* (Santa Monica: Rand Corporation, August 1982).

22. Kent H. Marquis, with the assistance of Patricia A. Ebener, *Quality of Prisoner Self-Reports: Arrest and Conviction Response Errors* (Santa Monica: Rand Corporation, March 1981). For a summary of a complex technical report, see pp. v–viii.

23. See Blackmore and Welsh, "Selective Incapacitation," 516–17, for a summary of Cohen's analysis.

24. John Monahan, *Predicting Violent Behavior: An Assessment of Clinical Techniques* (Beverly Hills: Sage, 1981).

7
The Dangerous Offender and the Endangered Criminal Justice System

The Overwhelmed System

Once upon a time, and not long ago, it was the fashion for criminologists to find reasons to deflate the popular anxiety about crime: We said that the data were erratic, that the *Uniform Crime Reports* were full of built-in errors that made the prevalence of crime seem worse than it was, that unusual political or economic conditions had brought about an abnormal but temporary increase in the crime rate, or that there were artifacts in the statistics that heightened public apprehension about crime beyond warrant. Patience would be rewarded. Another year would show a dramatic fall in the incidence of crime, and everyone would feel sheepish about their exaggerated concern. Years have gone by, the crime rates have failed to drop, and sheepish criminologists have joined the general alarm.

Looking back, I suppose that some of our nonchalance was caused by the expert's long view. Social data tend to run in cycles, and criminological data might not be an exception. Many of us mistrusted the sources of our statistics. The self-serving possibilities inherent in the *Uniform Crime Reports* seemed likely to corrupt at least some of the reports submitted by police departments to the Federal Bureau of Investigation. Some criminologists of the left, in a misapplication of their ideology, argued that the crime problem was exaggerated by the capitalist press to divert attention from the crisis confronting the social and political system because of its contradictions.

Our cool reassurances soothed few of the laity. Ordinary citizens can read the widely published statistics of crime as well as the occupants of the nation's cloisters of learning. Those who live in our metropolitan areas, as most of us do, may have had the experience of a mugging, a burglary, or an auto theft. If they have not, friends and neighbors have had tales of such depredations to tell, all to be supplemented and reinforced by daily news stories of the harrowing experiences of other citizens whose possessions have been plundered and their lives altered by the random intervention of criminals. Beyond the routine accounts of routine crimes, there are frequent and genuine horrors: mass murders, serial murders, gruesome acts of murderous sadism, and callous rapes of unprotected and vulnerable women and girls. A commitment to scientific rigor might justify the dismissal of such incidents as merely anecdotal evidence of increasing disorder, not to be accepted as widely true. This is a view that only the most detached criminologists and passionate young ideologues are prepared to accept. To minimize the danger in our city streets is to fly in the face of the reality of crime itself as well as the reality of the public response.

Consider the most common violent offense, the unskilled crime of robbery. According to the *Uniform Crime Reports* for 1982, there were 536,890 muggings of various kinds, armed and unarmed, on the street or in a home or store, committed in the country. That was a decline of 6 percent from 1981 and a legitimate occasion for modest official rejoicing.[1] Those half-million muggings were 152,672 more than took place in 1973—an increase of 39.7 percent. The rate of robbery has gone from 183.1 per 100,000 population in 1973 to a peak of 250.6 per 100,000 in 1981 and 231.9 in 1982. In the Standard Metropolitan Statistical Areas, (SMSA), in which three-quarters of all Americans live, the robbery rate per 100,000 is 298.6. That average conceals some even more disturbing extremes. In New York state, the robbery rate for all the SMSA's was 674.7, in California, 388.3, in the District of Columbia, 1,494.5.[2]

The trend for the other crimes of violence is about the same. From what seemed at the time to be an intolerably high rate in 1973, the incidence sailed up by about a third. In 1973 the rate for all index violent crimes was 417.4 per 100,000. In 1982 that rate was 555.3, an increase of 33 percent.

These figures are vaguely familiar to the casual news reader or television viewer. No one should be surprised at the swelling anger they have aroused. Legislators have tried to meet the demand for solutions with simple and obvious statutes that increase the penalties imposed on street criminals. In some states, juvenile court jurisdiction has been removed for minors accused of violent crimes. In many other states, juvenile courts waive jurisdiction for older youths, binding them over for prosecution in a criminal court. Prison sentences have been lengthened, mandatory minimum sentences have been prescribed for many violent offenses in a number of states, and for the particularly abhorrent offenses the sentence of life without possibility of parole may be imposed. The clamor for the resumption of the death penalty has been met by a dribble of executions, which will surely increase to a spate as avenues of appeal come to an end for the men and women waiting on condemned rows.

These measures are an understandable response to the demand that something must be done. The only influence the state can bring to bear on the crime rates is through changes in how it administers criminal justice. The trend toward increasing severity will continue, though how much farther no one can predict. In spite of the national fancy for systems analysis and operations research leading to an acceptable balance between costs and benefits, an orderly solution is not in sight.

The prospect for grave damage to the criminal justice system is real and serious. The police are expected to carry out impossible tasks, and they cannot meet that expectation. Clearance rates for robbery in 1982 were about 25 percent nationally, for burglary, about 15 percent.[3] There is good reason to believe that most of the really persistent criminals are eventually caught, but before they are booked they have made numerous "scores" against the public and enjoyed successive victories over the police before their capture and ultimate defeat.[4]

Although public support for the police is firm among the comfortable, and sympathetic understanding of their inability to accomplish all that is expected of them is general, neither technology, training, nor increases in personnel are likely to improve the clearance rates. Among the uncomfortable classes, which receive the most police attention, neither support nor understanding is increasing. This state of affairs has existed for a long time, long before data on clearance rates or studies of police/community relations became so abundant. It is a condition that, because it does not improve, becomes steadily worse. In an environment of endemic criminal violence, the worsening condition widens the community cleavage. For the poor, the police have never been seen as a service. The police response to violence, however reasonable and temperate it may seem to the middle classes, will seem increasingly oppressive and unreasonable to those classes that produce street crime.

Plea-bargaining for all but the gravest offenses has become standard in large jurisdictions and more common than not in smaller communities. We rationalize the process and search for benefits other than clear court dockets and economical litigation, but the potential for injustice is obvious. The pressures to short-cut the due process of the law are irresistible. Given the procedural traditions of criminal justice and the limited resources available for its administration, negotiation of charges and sentences is considered a necessity in all but the most peaceful jurisdictions.[5]

In spite of the convincing justification of negotiated justice, the prospect for long-range damage is gloomy. Our national indulgence in the practice has brought us close to the eventual abandonment of the traditional adversary system, with its promise of a day in court for even the most obviously guilty defendant. The institutionalization of these negotiations in statutory law is not far off. Gradually the presumption of guilt will be standardized in criminal litigation, a long step toward the police state.[6]

Penologists argue inconclusively whether our prisons and jails are worse than ever before, an unprofitable debate that will never be settled to the satisfaction of either side. What is certain is that they are nasty, dangerous, larger, and more crowded than ever before in the history of the nation. The flow of spoiled humanity into our penitentiaries and juvenile "training schools" has begun to convert these warehouses into human rubbish piles.

As our criminal codes become more stringent, this condition will worsen. We are cramming an increasingly heterogeneous population of offenders, many inflamed with racist furies, into prisons designed long ago for more tractable convicts who could be controlled by procedures that are no longer practical, even if they were ethically acceptable in contemporary American culture. In the larger states prison populations fall into grotesquely disproportionate racial distributions. Because of our preoccupation with criminal violence, a large and ever-increasing percentage of prisoners are men who have been convicted of violent crimes. Most of them are accustomed to violence and use it to settle their problems. They have created a culture of intimidation in the disintegrating prison community.

It is no wonder that destructive riots are a recent memory and a constant anxiety to administrators of prison systems. The drift to disaster is a powerful current. It will not be suddenly reversed, but measures for damage control can still be taken. It is a gigantic irony that the dangerous offender is endangering the whole system of criminal justice with all that that system means for fairness and democracy.

The Underclass and Violent Crime

Further decline in the crime rate is to be expected, though not to the supposedly halcyon level of 1973, let alone the mythical domestic peace that many Americans believe to have been general in a distant past. The men born during the baby boom of the 1950s are approaching their forties, about the usual age of retirement from criminal careers except for the most dedicated practitioners. A declining birth rate will produce fewer young people for schools and universities and fewer criminals for prisons and jails. The youth culture of the 1960s and 1970s, which throbbed with rebellion and nodded with dope, has aged into bourgeois tranquillity. The comfortable youth of America in the 1980s are no longer aggrieved. It follows that if the violence of the 1960s and the 1970s was partly caused by the rebellion of the middle-class young, we can now expect a respite from that source of urban disorder.[7]

There is plenty of reason to suppose that the rate of violence will stabilize not far below its present level. Although our youths are in general docile, the social structure contains new sources of conflict. The U.S. novelty is the underclass. It comprises the structurally unemployed, men and women who are never regularly employed and must survive on welfare payments or by their wits. The underclass is disproportionately, but by no means wholly, composed of blacks and various Hispanics. Their options are few. Some women can make a career out of welfare, a support system that is not readily open to men. Prostitution, gambling, and the narcotics trade will support others of both sexes. The attractions of the "index" crimes will draw the more daring into felony careers, thereby escaping for a while not only the penury of the underclass but also its ennui.

There is no firm estimate of the number of youths trapped in the underclass. Official statistics are suggestive. We are learning to think of an unemployment rate of 7 percent as normal, with the rate for black youths hovering close to 50 percent. The periodic release of this data is usually accompanied by the cautionary statement that they represent those persons in the national work force who are actively seeking jobs. Some of these people are underclass, but the solid mass are those who survive outside the normal labor market, seldom or never seeking work within it. In a recent survey of this problem, Kornblum observed that the 1980 census counted some 32 million persons as "impoverished" and that "of this number, perhaps 9 million would be considered 'underclass' because of chronic unemployment, long-term welfare dependency, criminal careers, and deinstitutionalized patient status."[8]

It is a matter of speculation whether the underclass is growing or not and, if it is, how fast. It is numerous enough to supply the nation with a large pool of unskilled felons and potential felons, ready to take up a career of thuggery, handy with pistols or knives, and not deeply concerned with the consequences of apprehension.

Together with the more traditional varieties of criminals, this pool of offenders and potential offenders will keep the criminal justice system occupied at its present level of activity—at least, for many years to come. The prevention of street crime at the source must depend on the dissolution of this class of chronically redundant but able-bodied men and women and their children—a challenge that U.S. society has long ignored at its increasing peril.

The purposeful disposition of underclass street criminals, once they are caught and convicted, is the insoluble problem confronting the nation's courts and penal apparatus. With so little to lose, the dispossessed are not readily deterred by the sanctions of the law, nor do the behavioral sciences offer nostrums that promise their reconciliation to a peaceable acceptance of their lot.

It is a problem for which no prospect of a solution is to be seen. Young men and women of the underclass are without skills. There are no incentives that are credible to them—or, for that matter, to anyone else—to learn a simple skill that would qualify them for a place in the labor market. They lack the discipline and often the physical strength to work as unskilled laborers—even if the economy's need for strong backs did not dwindle with each innovation supplied by an increasingly resourceful technology. The armed services, which used to need large numbers of healthy but not necessarily educated or even educable young men, have long since passed the stage where such recruits can be used. If pessimism about the future of street crime needs a warrant, the condition and prospects of the underclass indicate that street criminals will be on the streets for a long time to come.

Marxists and the Underclass

Marxists have no difficulty explaining the underclass or the drift of so many of its numbers into felony careers. Marx himself, in a vivid passage in *Capital*, referred to it as the *lumpenproletariat*, comprising the casualties of the capitalist economy from whom thieves, prostitutes, and vagabonds would be recruited.[9] Responsible radical criminologists firmly reject the romantic notions that some of the sillier Marxists have entertained concerning the criminal class as the vanguard of socialist revolution. Turning back to the writings of Marx and Engels, they find plenty of authority for the assertion that, far from useful soldiers in the struggle against capitalism, the constituents of the "stagnant" *lumpenproletariat,* when "habituated to a criminal life-style" are destructive to revolutionary progress.[10]

Criminologists of the left who are closer to the squalor and despair of the underclass are much more specific about the foolishness of their colleagues who sentimentalize street criminals at a safe distance. In a recent English perspective on crime as an inevitable consequence of capitalism, Lea and Young engage in the customary denunciations of capitalist injustice, but then go on to observe that in the inner cities of a modern industrial state social and economic hopelessness create a Hobbesian war of all against all. It is the poor who prey on each other:

> Crime is the end-point of a continuum of disorder. It is not separate from other forms of aggravation and breakdown. . . . It is streets you do not dare walk down at night, it is always being careful, it is a symbol of a world falling apart. It is lack of respect for humanity and for fundamental human decency.[11]

For Lea and Young, crime is the product of a culture saturated with the bitterness of relative deprivation, the sense that the exclusion from opportunity that permeates the community is incomprehensibly unfair. In England, as in the United States, the working class and the underclass alike are no longer insulated and unaware of the conditions of affluence.[12] These writers argue for a "left realism" embodying accountability of the police to the community that is policed, the "reintegration" of the offender through community-based sanctions wherever possible, and the use of prison only where no other alternative is feasible.[13] Whether this reorientation of criminal justice will lighten the burden of crime in the inner cities remains to be seen. The themes are familiar, if the orchestration is new.

None of this new-found radical concern about law and order addresses the social and economic influences that create the underclass, most of which—racism, the new technology, the export of unskilled jobs to the Third World—have little or nothing to do with the crises of the capitalist political and economic system. It is difficult to believe that the more purposeful penology recommended by these authors will be more effective in socializing underclass criminals than our present aimless methods. The reconciliation of the dispossessed to their hopelessness calls for a purposeful concern that no one can see in the distance. The crisis requires more strenuous efforts to bring the underclass back into the social structure where it belongs.

Approaches to the Control of Dangerous Offenders

To set aside a class of offenders as *dangerous* and therefore to be sentenced as such calls for a sacrifice of due process on the utilitarian altar. The future violence of offenders cannot be predicted without making an unacceptable number of mistakes. In chapter 6, we saw that the Greenwood/Abrahamse model of "selective incapacitation"—which is based on prediction by the statistical manipulation of personal characteristics as an aggregation of binary variables—must produce a high percentage of false-positive and false-negative errors, perhaps as high as 50 percent. It may be argued that these variables would never be summed up for anyone but a convicted criminal, whose violation of the law should deny him the right to protest. That argument fails, first because of its unfairness: A man should never be labeled as something which he is not, no matter how unworthy a man he may be. Second, to install incarcerative controls for protracted periods of time for supposedly dangerous offenders will be a prodigious expense and one wasted on those who are incorrectly assessed as dangerous. Third, and perhaps most important, no one has proposed a plan for what is to be done with the dangerous offender once he is under lock and key. How long will he be kept apart from the rest of us? What will he do while in custody? Tagged as *dangerous*, what assurance will he have that he will not also be regarded as hopeless?

There is an even more fundamental objection. As it has been practiced in English-speaking countries, the criminal law has gradually created a system for discovering the truth about the commission of a criminal offense. Although the system is impressive as a theoretical model, its practice falls distressingly short of perfection. Nevertheless, its aim is the establishment of the truth about an event. Its commitment to fairness is explicit in principle and practice, regardless of its violations by all the participating parties.

It has never done well at assigning individuals to a status. The sentencing process is cluttered with opportunities for the expression of judicial idiosyncrasy and prejudice. Agreement on criteria for decision-making has never been as general as the consensus on trial and appellate procedures. For centuries there has been a struggle to define the grounds for diminishing responsibility for an offense on account of mental impairment. To this day a solution satisfactory to the legal and the medical profession is still sought, even though there is a general consensus among orthodox psychiatrists as to the diagnostic criteria for most psychoses and other mental disorders. After nearly a century for special treatment for juvenile offenders, there is a disintegrating consensus on who may be treated as a child with diminished responsibility for his acts. Once the decision has been made in the child's favor, we are even less certain as to what we should do about him or her.

As to dangerousness there is not even a consensus that the concept is admissible. None of the professions concerned with the administration of justice have settled on a definition of the term, to say nothing of the criteria by which a dangerous offender can be distinguished from other offenders who are occasionally or never violent. It is perfectly respectable to deny that dangerousness is a concept that should have any standing in the law.

To advocate a rickety statistical support for decisions to apply so debatable a concept to an individual offender is to place the claims of social science technology above the administration of due process to the defendant at the bar. That position raises serious questions about the moral and intellectual perspectives of those who urge predictive methods on the judiciary. High technology should be administered by cooler heads, even with respect to the fear in the streets.

In chapter 2, the work of Floud, Young, and the Working Party on Dangerousness was summarized. Eschewing predictive methods, this British group decided on the infliction of "grave harm" as the distinguishing characteristic of the dangerous offender.[14] Their proposals dismiss the predictive methods fancied by U.S. criminologists—even though the methods of prediction now preferred in the United States received their first administrative trials in Britain under the direction of Hermann Mannheim and Leslie Wilkins, two of that nation's most eminent social scientists.[15]

It is important to read the Floud/Young proposals in the context of the Working Party's consensus on the state of criminal sanctions in the United Kingdom. One consistent theme in their considerations is the perspective that the use of prisons is excessive. Many prisoners should not have been sent to prison at all, and most of those whose crimes require a sentence to confinement should serve shorter terms. If the sentencing structure is to be modified, changes in fundamental policy should not be piecemeal: The whole structure should be thought of as an equilibrium not to be disturbed at any point without considering the consequences at all other points. If special provision for the control of the dangerous offender is needed, such an innovation should not be enacted into law without careful attention to its probable effects on the rest of the criminal justice system. To achieve rationality in sentencing, improvements in the control of the violent offender should be installed as a part of the fundamental revision of the criminal code.

This perspective calls for realism. No reductions in the penalties for ordinary offenders are likely without exceptions for certain kinds of offenders: that is, those who commit acts of "grave harm." Rather reluctantly, I infer, Floud and Young and their colleagues conceded that the community must be given special protection from such persons, but their incapacitation should only be as long as necessary within the limit of the determinate sentence imposed by the court. The Working Party refused to have any truck with predictive devices, preferring to rely on the trial judge to decide the length of the sentence, subject to automatic review by the Court of Appeal.

Reliance on the judiciary has the disadvantage of reposing confidence in judges who, in Britain, sometimes err on the side of excessive punitiveness. Nevertheless, there is a consistency here with the traditions of the common law. If there is to be the innovation of a "protective sentence," no legislation can be written that will provide for all the unforeseen contingencies in its application. It is well to require the judiciary to take responsibility for its interpretation, case by case, subject to remedial intervention by Parliament to allow for correction of judicial trends when they appear to depart too far from the public will. Obviously, this process cannot move without a lot of controversy, often heated but always wholesome and to be expected in a democratic polity.[16]

The general principles of the Floud/Young proposals are simple, pragmatic, and conservative. First, the court may impose a "protective sentence" on an offender only if he or she has on a previous occasion committed an offense in the category of "grave harm," and if the instant offense is also of such a nature. Second, the court must assure that advice from the police, psychiatrist, and a probation officer is received and considered—though not necessarily followed. Third, the offender is to be given the right of notice that he may be sentenced protectively and his right of appeal is assured. Fourth, although he must serve a part of his sentence in prison, he is to be released "on license" as soon as a judgment can be made that such a release would be safe. Fifth, while he is under sentence in the community he is always to be under probation or after-care supervision.

These proposals are consistent with the historical evolution of the criminal law. They concede that offenders who persist in serious crime must be restrained, but they require that the courts should determine who they are, one by one, in accordance with specific statutory directives. If there are to be false-positives—and inevitably there will be some, even though no one can ever know who they are—they will occur only after individual consideration of the situation of the offender who has been found guilty of a crime of such seriousness as to call for an extended sentence. Automatic appeal will protect both the offender and the community from the imposition of excessive sentences by impulsive judges, and at the same time valuable case law will be created. If new criminal justice policy is needed for dangerous offenders, the Working Party has pointed the way to legislation that will protect the rights of the offender as well as the rational development of the law.

The Present Disarray in the United States

Our habitual criminal laws, legacies from a time when thought about criminal sanctions was much more casual than now, are still on the books. As I concluded in a brief review in chapter 2, and as Sleffel showed in her much more comprehensive study, they are mostly honored in disuse.[17] Except in a few southern states, notably Texas, where severity assumes primacy over other values, these laws are infrequently invoked. They are of some value, I suppose, in plea-bargaining, but as a protection against the dangerous offender they have long outlived their usefulness, if they ever had any. The severe sentences provided in every criminal code for the major crimes of violence assure that the repetitively violent criminal can be incarcerated for as long as need be, and often much longer. The resort to these statutes for the prolonged confinement of lesser property offenders, marijuana pushers, and other such nuisances is either an abuse of judicial power or a demonstration of outright judicial incompetence. Such grotesque disproportionality should have been outlawed long ago in the combined interests of justice and economy.

The model statutes drafted by the American Bar Association and the American Law Institute in the 1960s have not been much more successful. The federal government adapted the Model Penal Code section on dangerous offenders proposed by the American Bar Association in 18 U.S.C.A. 3575 (19   ). At the time of this writing, Congress has yet to enact statutes placing into force an entirely new criminal code. Four states—Hawaii, New Hampshire, North Dakota, and Oregon—have also adapted the Model Penal Code. Their provisions were summarized by Sleffel.[18]

The larger states continued their status quo until the late 1970s, when public concern about street crimes reached a point at which the demand for legislative action could no longer be evaded. Three types of legislation have been adopted to meet the problem, no one of them entirely incompatible with the others. These strategies are mandatory sentencing, determinate sentencing, and guideline sentencing. Because each of these general sentencing policies will influence the nature and duration of the control of offenders considered to be threats to the public safety, something should be said here about them. I shall draw on the excellent review prepared by the Panel on Sentencing published under the auspices of the National Academy of Sciences.[19]

Mandatory Sentencing

The mandatory minimum sentence has been widely advocated by commentators and impromptu critics who have given little thought to the extensive experience with such policies that has accumulated over the last two or three centuries. In an exhaustive review, Cohen and Tonry observe that

> As under any severe but rigid rule, sympathetic cases cause decision makers to seek ways to avoid the rule. Juries, judges, and lawyers have routinely evaded mandatory sentencing laws for 300 years.[20]

The object of such sentences is deterrence. In the sixteenth, seventeenth, and eighteenth centuries this abstract aim was easy enough to enact in the halls of Parliament, but hard to apply to a living, breathing defendant found guilty of the capital crimes of sheep-stealing, poaching, or pocket-picking for which the law unambiguously required the gallows. Common sense did not prevail over the strenuous objections of the precedent-bound judiciary until the law reforms of the nineteenth century, when Sir Samuel Romilly and other legislators convinced Parliament that a sentencing policy that forced acquittals of the guilty in the interest of common humanity could not possibly accomplish the purposes of the criminal law.[21]

The modern mandatory sentences do not approach the ferocity of prereform English criminal laws. But in U.S. courts where laws may mandate life sentences for repetitive felonies, often including property offenses or minor roles in the narcotics traffic, common sense overrules the legislation, and pleas to lesser charges are allowed, sometimes in spite of provisions that are intended to rule out such negotiations.

For the serious crimes of violence, mandatory sentences are redundant. First-degree murderers will receive life sentences, or occasionally in states allowing the death penalty, they will be executed. In most states second-degree murderers will be sentenced to long terms in prison, assuring their confinement for many years regardless of either the mitigating circumstances of the crime or any remissions for good behavior while incarcerated.

Along with a few other states, California has put into active use a sanction that has long been in the statutes but that has hitherto been infrequently invoked: life without possibility of parole. Subject to some restraining procedures, a governor might pardon such a convict or commute his sentence to a less rigid term of servitude, but the motivation to do so will seldom inspire an elected official. Prison disciplinarians are already perplexed by the accumulation of hundreds of violent criminals serving sentences that can only end when they die. It is hardly realistic to remind convicts serving terms that deny them a prospect of release that however distant its realization may be, hope can be kept alive by compliance with rules and blameless behavior.

Dangerous offenders are men and women who have committed repeated offenses calling for extended incarceration. No mandatory minimum sentence is needed to assure that outcome of their trial, rasonable severity should be built into the law. That is an attainable goal, given legislative care to provide for sensible flexibility in sanctions. The futility of severe mandatory minimum sentences for offenders who have not committed violent crimes will become evident to legislators when they are confronted with continually rising appropriations for minimum prison maintenance.

Determinate Sentencing

The revival of determinate sentencing in U.S. criminal justice represents the triumph of the so-called justice model of penology over the waning influence of the rehabilitative ideal.[22] Dissatisfaction with the pretensions of parole boards in the administration of the indeterminate sentence had become widespread in the 1970s—so general that an unlikely coalition of liberals and hard-line conservatives joined to topple the system in states as different from each other as California, Minnesota, Indiana, and Maine. In its place a system of determinate sentencing has been established whereby convicts are sentenced by the court to a fixed term, subject only to some remission for good behavior. When sentencing, a judge in most states may augment (or as a new usage would have it, "enhance") or reduce the term to be served according to his opinion of the factors that might justify increased severity or leniency.[23] In California a judge must aggravate or mitigate within limits prescribed in the statute. When he decides to do either, he must make his reasons a matter of record. Where a prisoner is sentenced to a life term, his release on parole is determined by a new board of prison terms, one of whose principal duties is fixing the time of parole for lifers.

Blumstein and his colleagues on the Panel of Sentencing have reviewed the consequences of the determinate sentencing upheaval.[24] Their cautious conclusion is that the increases in prison populations that accompanied the adoption of determinate sentencing were largely the continuation of trends toward increased punitiveness that had been under way for several years prior to these legislative changes. These trends are clearly discernible in the statistical reports of the last decade, and they have continued up to the present time. Because legislatures are still responding to public pressures for still more punitiveness, and because their responses are engraved in fixed sentences from which judges cannot deviate far, we must expect that the disgraceful crowding of U.S. prisons will continue for some time to come. It is heartening to observe, however, that some legislators are beginning to see the advisability of a look at population projects before they make further upward adjustments of sentencing policy.[25]

Because of the well-established statistical capability of the California Department of Corrections, numerous studies of the switch in that state from indeterminate to determinate sentencing have been done. They have been summarized by Cohen and Tonry in a comprehensive review of the impact of sentencing reform.[26] Generally, it was noted that a number of legislative changes converged at about the same time to increase the use of prisons during the late 1970s. However, once the data were disentangled so far as possible, it appeared that determinate sentencing had slightly reduced the length of prison terms for most offenses but that offenders committing lesser felonies had been more frequently committed to prison than under the indeterminate sentencing laws. This peculiar result was due to the drastic change in the probation subsidy laws rather than a necessary consequence of determinate sentencing. The authors agree with Blumstein's conclusion that the trends toward increased prison use had been going on for several years before the statutory change.

Sentencing policy can be made by a legislature, but experience shows that results are suspect when a topic so vulnerable to demagoguery is settled in such a forum. Even with best intentions, the legislature and its committees lack the time and staff required to pay continuous attention to the details of a sound policy and to monitor its execution. The ascendant hard line is impatient with data and eager for the approbation of a poorly informed and anxious public. The better solution, now adopted in Minnesota, Oregon, and Washington, is to delegate the formulation and review of sentencing policy to a special commission appointed by the governor and charged with maintaining a balance between the protection of the public and a sound allocation of limited penal resources.

Guideline Sentencing

The United States Parole Commission was one of the earliest decision-making authorities to look to social science for assistance in arriving at consistency in sentencing. Aware of the promise of the computer in organizing data and reporting experience in categories, the commission arranged with three jurimetric criminologists—Don M. Gottfredson, Leslie T. Wilkins, and Peter B. Hoffman—to transpose its files to computer disks for rapid reference. Originally the plan was to develop experience tables somewhat like those in use by insurance actuaries. In this way a table might reveal to a commission member reviewing the case of a recidivist auto thief what the outcome of decisions in like cases of auto thieves had been in the past.

Further consideration led the commission and the project staff to alter the strategy. It was decided that consistency required a close examination of experience in past decision-making so that a range of sentences for similar offenses could be provided for the guidance of decision-making commissioners and hearing officers. A simple grid was created (see table 7–1) that called for classifying an offender according to offense severity (from "Low" to "Greatest") and offender "characteristics" (from "poor" to "very good" depending on the statistical assessment of the risk of recidivism). Sentence ranges for each intersection on the grid were described in terms of the past decisions of the commission. Thus, an offender convicted of a "Greatest Severity II" crime (the most serious offenses in the classification system) who was rated "Very Good" as to risk of recidivism might be sentenced at the same range as another offender whose crime was rated "Very High" as to severity (two steps lower than Greatest Severity II) but "Poor" as to risk of recidivism.

This is a system of *descriptive* guidelines, and its object is to

Table 7–1
United States Parole Commission Guidelines
Recommended Months of Incarceration before Release on
Parole (Adult Offenders)

	Offender Characteristics			
Offense Severity	Very Good	Good	Fair	Poor
Low	0–6	6–9	9–12	12–16
Low moderate	0–8	8–12	12–16	16–22
Moderate	10–14	14–18	18–24	24–32
High	14–20	20–26	26–34	34–44
Very high	24–36	36–48	48–60	60–72
Greatest I	40–52	52–64	64–78	78–100
Greatest II	52 +	64 +	78 +	100 or more

Source: *U.S. Parole Commission Rules, Section 2–20*, U.S. Department of Justice, Washington, D.C., 1 September 1981.

guide the Parole Commission toward consistency in sentencing. Nothing in the concept requires the commission to observe the guidelines in any specific case, but in the decade of experience that has been accumulated compliance has been high. The retributive intent of the system is implemented in the rating of offenses according to severity, and the incapacitative intent is effected in the rating of risk. It is a system that depends on the codification of past experience but will lend itself to some adjustment according to the assessment of the results. Because of impending changes in the federal criminal laws, drastically modifying the administration of parole, the future use of these guidelines must be in some doubt, but it remains the model for sentencing by voluntary reference to past experience.[27]

It is a model that preserves tradition and resists innovation. As Fisher and Kadane argue in an elegant article, there are several serious objections to their application. First, they are "unthoughtfully conservative"—that is, they maintain that what has always been done has always been just, which is not necessarily true. Second, if, as probably has been the case in most sentencing structures, race has been a partial determinant of sentences, then an ethical decision has to be made as to how and in what ways the guidelines are to be "purged" of that factor. Shall the guidelines provide that blacks shall be treated exactly as whites were treated in the past, or shall the purging follow a different rule? Third, the specification of the salient factors—severity and risk characteristics—is open to error, both by intentional bias and by misapprehension. In short, they "[substitute] statistical sophistication, which is useful but not essential, for ethical sophistication, which is critical."[28]

The alternative to the descriptive guidelines developed by Gottfredson and his colleagues is the guideline by *prescription*, the paradigmatic example of which is the Minnesota model, presented in table 7–2. Here, the goal is to develop a completely retributive sentencing structure, relying on a grid that takes into consideration only the seriousness of the offense and the criminal history.

This two-dimensional grid limits judges to the range of terms provided in each cell, except where "substantial and compelling reasons" (these reasons to be specified as part of the record of conviction and sentence) call for a judge to mitigate or aggravate the sentence beyond the range indicated. The compliance of the sentencing judges with the guidelines is under continuous review by a Sentencing Guidelines Commission, consisting of the chief justice of the supreme court, or his designee, two lower court judges appointed by the chief justice, the commissioner of corrections, the chairman of the parole board, a prosecutor and a public defender, and two citizen members appointed by the governor. The commission is charged with establishing a presumptive fixed sentence based on the characteristics of the offense and the offender. In the construction of this sentencing prescription, it was important that the commission should not allow the capacities of state and local correctional resources to be exceeded. A research and statistical staff was provided to assure that experience was under continuous examination and that projections could be made to determine the effect of the changes in sentencing policy on prison and community corrections populations.

In principle, the comission is intended to be independent and to make its decisions without regard to political considerations. Obviously, as a creature of the governor, the legislature, and the supreme court, the commission may eventually be vulnerable to pressures to modify its decisions for reasons other than those mandated in the statute. So far, these pressures do not seem to have been applied: The commission has modified the guidelines in its 1983 review to provide for some reduction of the ranges in the grid.[29] The general consensus of criminal justice reformers and critics is heavily in favor of the well-insulated guidelines commission. It assures equity in the disposition of offenders, it provides for continuous review of experience, and it keeps politics out of the changing demands on the system. Although I heartily agree that the establishment of such a commission is a foundation stone for rationality in sentencing, it is also a formidable obstacle to truly innovative change. It is in the nature of independent commissions in other fields to administer

Table 7-2
The Minnesota Sentencing Grid: Sentences in Months, Determined by Severity of Offense and Criminal History

Severity Levels of Conviction Offense		Criminal History Score						
		0	1	2	3	4	5	6 or more
Unauthorized use of motor vehicle Possession of marijuana	I	12[a]	12[a]	12[a]	15	18	21	24
Theft-related crimes ($150 to $2,500) Sale of marijuana	II	12[a]	12[a]	14	17	20	23	27 25–29
Theft crimes ($150 to $2,500)	III	12[a]	13	16	19	22 21–23	27 25–29	32 30–34
Burglary—Felony intent Receiving stolen goods ($150 to $2,500)	IV	12[a]	15	18	21	25 24–26	32 30–34	41 37–45
Simple robbery	V	18	23	27	30 29–31	38 36–40	46 43–49	54 50–58
Assault, second degree	VI	21	26	30	34 33–35	44 42–46	54 50–58	65 60–70
Aggravated robbery	VII	24 23–25	32 30–34	41 38–44	49 45–53	65 60–70	81 75–87	98 90–104
Assault, first degree Criminal sexual conduct, first degree	VIII	43 41–45	54 50–58	65 60–70	76 71–81	95 89–101	113 106–120	132 124–140
Murder, third degree	IX	97 94–100	119 116–122	127 124–130	149 143–155	176 168–184	205 195–215	230 218–242

Source: Minnesota Sentencing Guidelines Commission (1981:23), Saint Paul, Minnesota.
Note: First degree murder is excluded from the guidelines by law and continues to have a mandatory life sentence.
[a]One year and one day.

honestly and rationally, but to leave the grand initiatives to other voices. In criminal justice, the innovations have tended to originate in the legislatures and the courts, both of which may be inclined to leave the vexatious maintenance of the sentencing structure to commissions charged with that function.

No one can deny the vast importance of rationality and equity in the administration of sanctions. My bias, as one whose experience has been mainly in the penological sector of the criminal justice front, is one of concern over what happens to the offender once he or she has had a sentence pronounced and must be hustled off to the state prison. What is certain is that the trend toward longer sentences for offenders considered dangerous will accumulate a mass of convicts that will be unmanageable within the perimeters of our maximum security penitentiaries. The Minnesota guidelines model, new and incompletely tested though it is, appears to promise the flexibility that will make possible an accommodation of severity to the resources on hand.

The urgency of innovative thought on this topic has been expressed before in this disquisition, and without repeating myself on the national disgrace of overcrowding, idleness, unplanned and unplannable administration of sanctions, the squalor and brutality of conditions in most prisons, and the nominal condition of probation and parole, I must now proceed to the consideration of a rational penology and the concepts from which it can be constructed.

Reason and Experience in Penology

The empirical tenor of the times has brought the nation to a recognition that our penal system requires a complete overhaul. For much too long the fascination of reformers has been drawn to the equivocal findings of evaluation researchers who sum up their entire statistical labors in two words: "Nothing works." It is as though the main issue to be settled in penology was the value of rehabilitative programs. Much more fundamental problems in the management of convicted offenders needed to be addressed, but they scarcely have been formulated.

The "nothing works" finding is beside any useful point, even if it were not based on research that was at best naive but usually slovenly. Instead of the uproarious concentration on the decline of the "rehabilitative ideal," our attention should have focused on a point at which two propositions of fundamental significance converge. Here they are in all their stark simplicity:

1. The nation's prison space is a costly resource that should never be squandered on any but those offenders whose danger to the community requires that they should be kept under firm and extended control.
2. When other means of adequate control are available, no purpose is served and much waste is incurred by incarcerating offenders who do not present a significant threat of physical violence to others.

These two propositions and their corollaries contain the basis for economy and effectiveness in the management of convicted offenders. Neither retributive nor utilitarian purposes are served by the present disposition of a minority of offenders in prison and the vast majority in conditions of nominal probation. At present our prisons contain too many offenders who shouldn't be there at all, too many who are released too soon, and an increasing number who are kept for years beyond any reasonable purpose for their confinement. At the same time, the nation maintains a system of probation and parole that at best is a well-meant ineffectuality, and too often a bad joke, a burlesque on the worst in U.S. bureaucratic habits.

Those of us who have been immersed in penological administration for long enough to see its grotesque anomalies have tried to make these two points for a good many years. Unfortunately, we haven't been able to make our voices heard over the din of debate on other criminal justice issues of more apparent interest to lawyers and sociologists. Our time has come, however: The cost of a prison cell goes up every year and so does the cost of guarding that cell. Further, under the prodding of the federal courts, there have been some tentative steps toward finding better ways of controlling offenders than cramming them indiscriminately into prisons like so much human rubbish. Not only is the time for an overhaul at hand, but the direction for change can be clearly seen.

Juvenile Justice and the Dangerous Offender

In chapter 3 we saw that the violent juvenile in Columbus is an unusual youth, one of a "violent few." We also saw that the juvenile courts are confronted with dilemmas that are even worse than they must seem to the judges who must resolve them. On the one hand, we have a substantial number of boys and girls, nearly 30 percent of our cohort, who commit violent offenses on one occasion only and are never heard from again. Some of their offenses were only technically violent—a purse snatching, a fistfight that went too far—while others were grave indeed, including some homicides. These offenders cannot be ignored, and there is every reason for the court to intervene decisively. With early delinquents, our data are clear enough that the intervention must be aimed at a planned return to the community as soon as that is possible. At the time of adjudication for the first serious offense, *the chances are better than they ever will be later in the youth's delinquent career for a successful termination of delinquency.*

What course of action should be taken? When the boy or girl is arrested for a serious crime, everything possible should be done to impress all concerned with the solemnity of the proceedings. Usually the child should be detained, the hearings in the juvenile court should be expedited, and in most such cases the disposition should provide for a period of incarceration. I have already said enough about the dangerously criminogenic conditions that prevail in too many of our penal facilities for youth so that it is needless to specify here in detail the requirements that they must be adequately staffed by well-trained and disciplined personnel, that programs of work and training must fill the day, that age groups must be kept separate, and that living units must be small and under expert supervision. But even if favorable conditions prevail in the training school, the first offender should not stay long. As soon as a satisfactory plan for his return to the community can be worked out, he should be paroled under planned and intensive supervision, with clearly understood consequences for infractions of the conditions of release.

There will be failures, but it is noteworthy that even under the far-from-optimal conditions that prevailed during the time of our study, the number of successes—that is, the singleton violent offenders—made up almost a third of our cohort. It does not require an optimist to conclude that that measure of success can be substantially increased with the commitment of maximum attention to the boy or girl in *serious* trouble for the first time. The expense may be considerable, but the savings to the community by terminating a delinquent career at its commencement rather than enduring its prolongation far into adulthood are attractive and obvious.

The recidivist juvenile offender presents a more difficult dilemma for constructive disposition. Where the new offense is not violent, there will be some leeway for installing the youth in a community program. Our data suggest that the prospects for further recidivism, whatever the disposition, are better than even. Nevertheless, the more restrictive the control, the sooner more recidivism can be expected. But if there is a second violent offense, there should be no question of an immediate return to the community. Beyond doubt, the firm control of a youth facility is required for a considerable period of time. The recidivist violent youth is a rare phenomenon, and it is well worth the investment of time, space, and professional control to assure that his return to the community is deferred until there is reason for confidence that he can comply with the requirements of intensive supervision.

Along with a number of other juvenile justice specialists, my colleagues and I were concerned with the question of "binding over" delinquents for trial as adult offenders. As I have previously noted, in New York this process has been legislated down to age 13 for youthful murderers and age 14 for other violent juveniles. At what age and by what criteria should the juvenile court waive jurisdiction for youthful violent offenders?

This question is not transcendently important. The much more important problem is what shall be done with the young offender once he has been tried and found responsible for a major felony. In many states he may be shoved into an adult prison in midadolescence, a disposition that may scare his peers remaining in the community but that can only create unpleasant and sometimes dangerous management problems for the prison authorities. That such a boy— or occasionally a girl—will usually survive the experience somehow is no cause for complacency. He will certainly be the worse for what happens to him, and his continued confinement will probably be required for a long time. Whether tried in an adult criminal court or a juvenile court, steps should be taken to assure that the disposition will be placement in a facility appropriate for his age. Later, he may be transferred to an adult prison when sufficiently toughened and matured.

To summarize, the violent juvenile offender must be the object of discriminating attention from the time of his first arrest. The circumstances of the offense must be realistically appraised: *What antecedent events brought about the offense with which this juvenile is charged? What community resources can be mobilized to maintain control and foster such changes in his or her situation as may be indicated?* If incarceration can be avoided with safety to the community and the offender, then intensive probation supervision should be ordered. If incarceration is unavoidable, it should be for as brief a term as possible and directed to a speedy and safe restoration to the community.

It is an anomaly for the juvenile court to retain jurisdiction over a recidivist girl or boy felon of age 16 or older. As I have suggested earlier, the question of court jurisdiction is not nearly as important as some believe: The really significant question has to do with what happens to the boy or girl after the court has pronounced a sentence. If the choice of disposition is limited to a brutalizing state prison or nominal probation, the jurisdiction of the court pronouncing sentence is irrelevant however prudent its intentions may be. Lifelong damage may be done soon after the court is through with the case.

Throughout its history, the juvenile court movement has stressed the importance of specialized attention to the boy or girl in trouble with the law. At this time in an offender's career society has its best chance to abort a long, miserable, and costly criminal career. With juveniles who have committed serious violence, that career, unless terminated by wise influence and firm control, will be longer, more miserable, and far more costly than that of the ordinary petty criminal nuisance. We hear from the neoconservative side of the criminal justice dialogue that the safety of the community calls for a policy of severity and the requirement that young people be forced to face responsibility for their offenses. So far as it goes, I cannot quarrel with this hard and tough line. But the nation can expect only more trouble from the notions that severity is enough and that a sense of responsibility will ensue from rigorous application of the criminal law to offending minors. The ruling concept of the juvenile court, so often misapplied by uncomprehending or indifferent judges, is still correct. The best interest of the child in trouble is the best interest of society.

Criminal Justice and the Career of Criminal Violence

The findings of our two studies of adult violence in Columbus are bleak. If we are correct in our conclusion that a policy of incapacitation will significantly reduce violent crime only at a prohibitive cost in prison space and urban turmoil, there is little reason to expect that harsher laws will result in safer streets.

Our longitudinal review of the careers of violent offenders in Columbus gives us additional reasons for pessimism. It appears that after a first term in prison, recidivists are no longer particularly intimidated by the wretched experiences to be encountered in standard U.S. prisons. If they are to be released within the limits of the customary sentences, their supervision must be intensive for a considerable period of time, with strict enforcement of the conditions of release. Later in this chapter I shall return to this requirement.

Improvements in the tattered system of criminal justice will produce benefits worth the effort and the moderate costs, even if no dramatic reduction in the rates of violent crime can be expected. We concluded that both adult and juvenile justice must become clearly predictable. The consequences of wrongdoing must no longer be so uncertain as to be worth a criminal's gamble on the outcome of his offense. The evidence has never been assembled to prove that swift and certain justice will deter commensurately with the degree of swiftness and certainty, in spite of opinions to that effect expressed by criminologists from the time of Beccaria. A rigorously controlled test of this ancient hypothesis is obviously beyond practical research methodology.

Reluctant though an empiricist may be to accept an *a priori* proposition into his belief system, I see little reason to doubt that some offenders—who knows what proportion?—will be discouraged from serious crime as the prospect of arrest and incarceration become more certain. Whatever the exact truth of that inexact proposition may be, our data and the data of other investigations lead to the conclusion that the more settled the commitment to a criminal career and the more experience of prison a felon may have the less effective is the predictable punishment of a criminal act in his or her intimidation.[30]

As matters stand, arrest is probably beyond the level of an even wager only in the case of homicide. While conviction and incarceration of arrested robbers, rapists, and assaulters are highly probable consequences, nothing in our study or in any of the official statistics suggests that that probability is anything more than eventual. Before the offender arrives at the prison reception center, he will have opportunities to commit additional crimes, and the advantage of prosecutorial discretion often favoring him. He will have traversed a tortuous route through the courts in the course of which he will often learn to substitute self-pity for guilt and shame.

What to do? There seems to be little reason to believe that adding to police strength and technology will be productive. More experimentation in deployment may produce marginally better control. For example, in Minneapolis a special police unit presides over surveillance of the eight most serious offenders known to reside in that city. The entire department is alerted to the names and records of these men. The results are equivocal in meaning. Arrest and conviction after the commission of crimes has been swift and certain, but the crimes committed have not been prevented.

As an example of innovation, this experiment is novel enough, even though its usefulness may be more for the improvement of the public impression of police effectiveness than in the actual reduction of crime. But what is impressive is not its usefulness, but the fact that a police department has innovated. Throughout the criminal justice system the overload of work has paralyzed both administrators and critics. Crime reports must be cleared, court dockets must be moved, and prison populations must approximate but not exceed by too much the capacity available. These are urgent tasks. Their accomplishment does not improve the system, but it keeps it alive. From my enquiries, I heard few new ideas and was more frequently asked for my own. The mood was one of wan and distant hope: The changing demography would reduce the crime-committing age groups; an improved economy would reduce unemployment and the pressures on young people to do something to get money any way they could; eventually the persisting demand for narcotics would be diminished. I often heard that the kids were losing interest in marijuana and hard drugs.

My conclusion in the light of our own research, the research done by others, and the perspective of the expert community is that this nation is in for a long haul toward serious reduction of the rate of criminal violence. While it is true that there is in prospect a major demographic change with a sharp decline in the male population in the age 20 to 29 group, a closer look reveals that although there will be 1,377,000 fewer young men in 1990 than there were in 1983, there will be 108,000 *more* black males in that year.[31] Sadly, not much progress has been made in putting young black men to productive work, and every study such as ours shows the tragically disproportionate number of serious crimes committed by such individuals. There is every reason to suppose that if our patterns of punishment do not change, prison populations will continue at a high plateau, but the racial mixture will contain an even greater predominance of black convicts than we now see in our state prisons.

New Principles for Punishment and Control

The objective is to achieve fairness in the administration of punishment and firmness in the management of control. So far as it goes, the "justice model" as advocated by Fogel is a long step toward the fairness that should characterize criminal justice. Subject to some leeway for mitigation and aggravation, felons who commit the same crimes and have the same records of recidivism should be treated alike. The Minnesota guidelines express this general principle. I want to carry that practice a good deal farther through the innovation of intensive field control.

Intensive Field Control

I cannot claim this innovation as my own, although in earlier writing I have suggested that more stringent methods of supervision of violent offenders should be adopted.[32] Such methods are now operational in a few states, most notably Georgia, Alabama, and New Jersey. Because the Georgia experience with Intensive Probation Supervision (IPS) has been under development for a longer period than any other, with provision for careful evaluation, a brief account of its operation will identify the model for discussion.

Intensive Probation began in July 1982 with the explicit objective of diverting from state prisons as many offenders as could be safely managed in the community. To assure that firm control would be maintained and that the plan would be acceptable to the communities in which it would be put into effect, elaborate measures were devised to differentiate IPS from conventional probation services.

The procedure begins at the time of sentence to prison. The convicted defendant's case is reviewed by the local representative of the IPS Division of the Department of Offender Rehabilitation. If the offender meets the criteria for placement in IPS, he is interviewed to ascertain his willingness to submit to its fairly onerous requirements and his suitability for the program. The criteria first:

1. Offender is under sentence to the state prison for less than five years;
2. Priority is given for offenders convicted of nonviolent crimes;
3. No acceptable risk of violent crime is present if the offender is allowed to remain in the community;
4. Offender's case is not under appeal;
5. Offender does not have a history of chronic drug abuse;
6. Offender is not a probationer revoked for the conviction of a new crime;
7. Offender has no major medical or psychiatric problems.

If the offender meets the basic criteria, he or she will be interviewed to determine whether a plan for residence, employment, and supervision can be devised and to assure that there are no other reasonable objections to her or his continued presence in the community. If all is well, and if the offender agrees to the program, the IPS representative will submit the plan to the court for approval of a modification of the sentence to provide for IPS placement.

As I have said, the conditions are onerous far beyond the requirements of conventional probation. They provide for:

1. *Face-to-face contact.* At least five contacts are required per week, usually comprised of two home visits at night, one office visit, one weekend visit, and one on-the-job visit.
2. *Curfew.* Depending on work schedules a curfew is required, usually at 8:00 P.M.
3. *Local record check.* The probation officer is responsible for a weekly check of arrest records to assure that the offender has had no police contacts.
4. *Community service.* IPS probationers are required to perform at least eight hours per week of unpaid community service, more if temporarily unemployed.
5. *Employment.* Full-time employment is required.
6. *Payment of fees.* Depending on ability to pay, probationers are required to remit a fee ranging from $10 to $50 a month.

Supervising so demanding a program calls for a staffing pattern entirely different from what is normal in conventional probation. Caseloads are strictly limited to no more than twenty-five probationers supervised by a team consisting of a probation officer and a "surveillance officer." The probation officer will be a social worker with full credentials and special training for the unusual tasks to be undertaken. The surveillance officer will be a police officer or, sometimes, a correctional officer, trained and detailed for the daily tasks of checking the whereabouts and activities of the offenders assigned to the caseload. As an innovation in an innovation, four caseloads out of the thirty now in service have been increased from twenty-five to forty, with two surveillance officers assigned to the supervisory team.

The results are not spectacular, but reassuring. As of 31 December 1983, 575 offenders had completed the program, of whom 125 had violated probation and been sent on to prison—a failure rate of 21.7 percent. A more recent study (October 1984) tracked consecutive commitments to IPS for eighteen months. At the end of the first six months, there were forty-two failures out of total of 436 (9.5 pecent); at the end of twelve months, there were 282 cases, of whom sixty-five had "fallen" (23.1 percent). There were 108 who could be followed for eighteen months, of whom there were thirty failures (27.8 percent).[33] So far no violent crimes have been committed by IPS "clients."

Up to this time, IPS in Georgia and similar programs in other states have scrupulously avoided the inclusion of offenders with records of violent crime or even the impression of dangerousness. The conservative introduction of so radically different an innovation is natural and prudent. However, it seems to me that experience has been gained already that will enable planners to make a fundamental change in the disposition of offenders. It might be built on a structure something like the following.

IPS should be the disposition of choice for all property felons except the rare birds who prefer the privacy of a prison cell. Those who violate the terms of IPS should be subjected to extended terms with more rigorous conditions and incarcerated only in the event of repeated and defiant violations.

With rare exceptions, all felons convicted of violent offenses should serve a term in jail or prison, if only to maintain public confidence in a system that appears to afford a measure of leniency to persons guilty of life-threatening crimes. As soon as a minimum term is served, in many cases a long time, plans should be made for release under a program similar to IPS. The period of time to be served under these conditions will vary according to the circumstances and conduct of the offender, but the objective should be eventual restoration to the community as a self-sustaining citizen.

Many potential objections can be made to such a system, some of which I can anticipate here:

1. Criminals guilty of heinous crimes may be punished too leniently. This is possible, but may be prevented by due deliberation by decision-makers and statutory provisions limiting discretion, as for example the Minnesota Guidelines described earlier in this chapter. Nothing in this plan will prevent a judge from sentencing such offenders to very long terms of imprisonment where criminal justice policy appears to require unusual severity.
2. There will be considerable risk incurred by the public from the release of violent offenders, even under the rigorous supervision proposed. Again, the risk cannot be denied, but it is certainly minimized beyond the present situation in which violent offenders are released under conditions of parole in which supervision is no more than nominal. Under the proposed application of IPS to such offenders, technical violations will ordinarily result in a return to prison, a prospect to be clearly understood by the convict at the time of release.
3. The cost may be prohibitive. While the fees to be paid by persons serving under the IPS system will partially support the expense, it cannot be expected that this kind of supervision will come cheap. To the extent that it reduces prison populations and prevents or delays the cost of construction of new prisons, there

can be no question of the value of the program in reducing penal costs. The out-of-pocket cost of adding one prisoner to a maximum security population varies from state to state, but even at the present level of inflation does not amount to more than a few thousand dollars at most. But that prisoner as one of a thousand cell-less prisoners who must be provided for in a new prison will cost many thousands of dollars, sometimes over $20,000 a year. He will be housed in a cell that may cost the taxpayers as much as $100,000 to build. Compared to such surreal figures the cost of IPS will be almost trivial.

4. The IPS will succumb to eventual bureaucratization. If it is successful, IPS will eventually turn into an unwieldy bureaucracy with echelons of administration and supervision stretching upward from the surveillance officer on the street to district, regional, area, and statewide officeholders. The inevitability of this outcome is to be seen in the administrative expansion of almost every public service in the nation, and certainly correctional services have been outstanding examples of the creation of layers of lower, middle, upper-middle and top management. But this is not a problem unique to IPS to be solved before proceeding with its further implementation. The curse of overbureaucratization can be offset by strong and continuously innovative leadership, provision for which is a responsibility of elected executives.

The history of civilization has many dark chapters. One of the darkest and most discouraging is the administration of punishment to offenders. No other function of the state is intended to do harm to citizens. The test of the civilization of any nation lies in the limits that its laws impose on the harm that may be done to violators of those laws. In these times humanity everywhere has reason to know the horrors and the abuses that may be committed in the name of law enforcement. The United States has not been immune to the infection of barbarism in the name of social control. Our constitution and laws have been designed to prevent cruelty to offenders. We have outlawed torture and mutilation, and we have made the death penalty an exceptional sanction. Maintaining these limits honors our culture. We must do more to work within these limits to assure the safety of our citizens and the restoration to society of our offenders as constructive citizens themselves.

Also in the history of civilization is a running account of violence and predation by warped and sometimes wicked men and women. So far the enlightenment of the most advanced nations has not been enough to eliminate their crimes. The United States, as a nation that has suffered more than most from all sorts of crime, has reason to be angry. But anger solves no problems, nor does it even reduce their pain. It can and should mobilize attention to the requirement that our system of justice must be overhauled, piece by piece, element by element. There is much to preserve in our tradition of criminal justice and much to change in its practice. I hope that this book has shown that preserving our tradition depends on fundamentally modifying our practice.

Notes

1. Federal Bureau of Investigation, *Uniform Crime Reports, 1982* (Washington, D.C.: United States Department of Justice, 1983), 17.

2. *Ibid.*, 43, table 2. Some writers are inclined to minimize the seriousness of this crime, pointing out that most muggers are unarmed, few victims are seriously injured, and sometimes, as in a purse-snatching, nobody is even threatened. Further, the amounts involved are not great, nothing like the magnitude of some white-collar crime. Specious. Intimidation of citizens is intolerable conduct, especially when deadly force is implied, if not threatened or inflicted. The amounts involved may be trivial to the comfortable but are usually crucial to the poor, who are the most frequent victims of this contemptible offense. For a further discussion from the Marxist perspective of this misguided leftism, see John Lea and Jock Young, *What Is to Be Done about Law and Order?* (London: Penguin Books, 1984), 105–12.

3. I have calculated these rates from the *Uniform Crime Report, 1982*, table 4. Unfortunately, FBI practice has consolidated the SMSA's for each state into one set of figures, suggesting a homogeneity that surely is fictitious.

4. Charles Silberman has made this point, to my mind persuasively, in his *Criminal Justice, Criminal Violence* (New York: Random House, 1979), 75–86. The self-reported criminal histories reviewed by Jan and Marcia Chaiken in their *Varieties of Criminal Behavior* (Santa Monica: Rand Corporation, August 1982), suggest that the eventual capture of high-rate offenders may be the climax of a long series of offenses for which they were not apprehended and that account for the low police clearance rates for robbery and burglary. On my personal acquaintance with a large number of criminals, some of them fairly astute, it is difficult for me to believe that there are many uncaught violent predators so proficient at their criminal specialties that they invariably elude arrest. One characteristic that seems to stand out in the Chaikens' account is a quality of recklessness that would preclude indefinite immunity from arrest.

5. For an account of what happens when plea-bargaining is ruled out,

see Jacqueline Cohen and Michael H. Tonry, "Sentencing Reforms and Their Impacts," in Alfred Blumstein, Jacqueline Cohen, Susan E. Martin and Michael H. Tonry, eds., *Research on Sentencing: The Search for Reform*, vol. 2 (Washington, D.C.: National Academy Press, 1983), 310–28. This review focuses on the experience in Alaska, where plea-bargaining was prohibited by the attorney-general in 1975. Reviewing an evaluation completed in 1980, Cohen and Tonry conclude that "If rules are sufficiently clear, if internal management processes are used to monitor day-to-day decisions, and if prosecutors can withstand the complaints of defense counsel, the Alaska experience ought to be replicable" (p. 328). I am impressed that the authors found that despite the ban on plea-bargaining, "guilty pleas continued to flow in at nearly undiminished rates even when the state offered [defendants] nothing in exchange for their co-operation" (p. 321).

6. I do not doubt that some adjustments in the administration of criminal justice can be made without doing violence to its traditional concern for due process. For a proposal to remove minor criminal charges from the Canadian courts, see Peter H. Solomon, Jr., *Criminal Justice Policy: From Research to Reform* (Toronto: Butterworths, 1983), 79–94. Solomon draws on the West German procedural innovation of the *penal order*, which provides that driving offenses and minor property crimes that are punishable by a fine may be disposed of in an police instrument citing the charge, the evidence supporting the charge, and specifying the punishment to be imposed. In West Germany a penal order cannot result in imprisonment, and if the defendant wishes to contest it he may, without any risk that the penalty will be greater than that prescribed in the order. Solomon advocates the introduction of this procedure in Canada for driving offenses, public order offenses, theft under $200, and possession of marijuana. Determining the extent to which penal orders would relieve congestion in U.S. courts is beyond the scope of this book, but any well-planned innovation should be welcomed if it would remove trivia from the courts and make available time and personnel for attention to serious crime of the kind we are considering in this volume.

7. For a discussion of the implications of the decline of the youth culture, see Senator Daniel Moynihan's optimistic article, "Peace—" in *The Public Interest* (spring 1978): 14.

8. William Kornblum, "Lumping the Poor: What Is the 'Underclass'?," *Dissent* (summer 1984): 296. Kornblum remarks that the career criminal should not be counted as "underclass": He has used crime as a route out of that predicament. He prefers to "narrow the definition," restricting it to

> people who are clearly "below" the poor in that they cannot survive unharmed for any length of time by themselves, because they lack both material resources and the ability to organize their lives. . . . [T]hey would include the homeless indigent, severe alcoholics, drug addicts, runaway children, and at-large psychotics who are not stable criminals. . . . Criminals from poverty areas or elsewhere should

be thought of as part of the underworld, a shadow society that has its own class system. . . .

Kornblum's point is that many impoverished men and women are desperately trying to lead respectable lives though sealed off from most avenues of opportunity. I think that Kornblum's redefinition obscures the nature of the problem as it confronts those Americans who must survive outside the national security system of employment, insurance, and pensions. One way out is through upward mobility to a job and participation in the national security system. Talented underclass people sometimes emerge by that route. Another adaptation is subsidence into the derelict status to which Kornblum's narrowed definition would be restricted. Still another is the career of crime and hustling, at which, I think, very few succeed for very long, but through which more than a few become long-time clients of the criminal justice system.

9. Karl Marx, *Capital: A Critique of Political Economy*, 1867, translated by Eden Paul and Cedar Paul (London: J.M. Dent and Sons, 1930), 711.

10. In a recent and uncomfortable critique of the selective incapacitation model, Andrew von Hirsch observes that, "Greenwood's approach . . . simply disregard[s] or downgrade[s] justice considerations. Whether one finds that course acceptable depends on one's values." Exactly. In all the statistical modeling that ultramodern criminologists are doing, regard for values, any values other than a dubious prospect of crime reduction, evaporates as though so much excess steam. What cannot be programmed for the computer cannot be accepted as policy. I am reminded of Wittgenstein's hypnotic maxim, "Whereof one cannot speak, thereof must one be silent." A useful mantra for the empiricist, but hazardous indeed for a democratic society grown increasingly dependent on that of which the computer can speak. See Andrew von Hirsch, "The Ethics of Selective Incapacitation: Observations on the Contemporary Debate," *Crime and Delinquency* 20(2) (April 1984): 174–94.

11. Lea and Young, *What Is to Be Done about Law and Order?*, 55.

12. *Ibid.*, 227–30.

13. *Ibid.*, 266–67.

14. Jean Floud and Warren Young, *Dangerousness and Criminal Justice* (London: Heinemann, 1981). This volume is the final product of a Working Party of which Floud was the chairman and Young the secretary. The membership of the Working Party comprised many of the most distinguished criminologists and practicing officers of the criminal justice system in England, whose ideas were incorporated in this report. For convenience, however, I shall refer to it hereafter as "Floud and Young."

15. The long and essentially unproductive history of predictive methods as guides to the sentencing decision will not be recapitulated in this volume. However, the importance of Leslie T. Wilkins's contributions in popularizing predictive methods, and later in prescribing limits to their use, should be recognized at this point. His work on this problem first came to notice in Hermann Mannheim and Leslie T. Wilkins, *Prediction Methods in Relation to Borstal Training* (London: Her Majesty's Stationery Office, 1955). The methods described in this monograph were adapted for use in

parole prediction in California and elsewhere in the United States. Experience has substantially modified Wilkins's views on the administrative application of predictive methods. See Don M. Gottfredson, Leslie T. Wilkins, and Peter B. Hoffman, *Guidelines for Parole and Sentencing* (Lexington, Mass.: Lexington Books, 1978), 90: "Early prediction workers . . . could not understand why parole boards did not make use of the instruments they had provided. It is easy to fall into the trap . . . of thinking that the provision of other forms and more powerful . . . prediction methods will provide the answers."

16. Floud and Young, *Dangerousness and Criminal Justice,* 154–57. A recent letter from Mrs. Floud (June 1984) informs me that Parliament has not yet taken these proposals under consideration.

17. Linda Sleffel, *The Law and the Dangerous Criminal* (Lexington, Mass.: Lexington Books, 1977): 21–26.

18. *Ibid.,* 29–39.

19. Blumstein et al., *Research on Sentencing,* vol. 1, 184–224. See also in volume 2 the exhaustive review by Jacqueline Cohen and Michael H. Tonry, "Sentencing Reforms and Their Impacts," 1, 305–446, especially at 340–446.

20. *Ibid.,* vol. 2, 340.

21. Douglas Hay, Peter Linebaugh, John G. Rule, E.P. Thompson, and Cal Winslow, *Albion's Fatal Tree,* chap. 1, "Property, Authority, and the Criminal Law" (London: Allen Lane, 1975). Hay, the author of this chapter, shows that "most historians and many contemporaries argued that the policy of terror was not working. More of those sentenced to death were pardoned than were hanged. . . . [R]ather than terrifying criminals, the death penalty terrified prosecutors and juries, who feared committing judicial murder on the capital statutes" (p. 23). Our mandatory sentencing laws are not so extreme, but already enforcement of compulsory jail sentences for carrying unregistered firearms is applied by the courts where danger is sensed but evaded where no criminal inclinations are evident.

22. The "rehabilitative ideal" has become a cant term, supposedly referring to the penological practices and theories of the 1950s and 1960s. Its demise in the early 1970s was sealed by the publication of the well-known but seldom read volume produced by Douglas Lipton, Robert Martinson, and Judith Wilks, *The Effectiveness of Correctional Treatment* (New York: Praeger, 1975). While the "ideal" is often lamented, I do not think it can be said that much effort was committed to its achievement. U.S. criminal justice decision-making has always been more dedicated to the aims of retribution and incapacitation than to rehabilitation. Because rehabilitation seems much more noble an objective than any other justification of punishment, it has flourished in penological rhetoric though not in penological practice.

23. If credit must be given for the revolution that supplanted the indeterminate sentence with the determinate sentencing, much of it must go to David Fogel, whose oddly entitled ". . . We Are the Living Proof . . ." (Cincinnati: Anderson, 1975) attracted wide attention by its antinomy of the "justice model" and the "medical model" of penology—with unsparing endorsement of the former and equal disdain for the latter. A year earlier,

Norval Morris's *The Future of Imprisonment* (Chicago: University of Chicago Press, 1974), had set the stage for this drastic change of direction with the author's customary elegance and rigor. For a still useful survey of the battleground, see *Determinate Sentencing: Reform or Regression?* (Proceedings of the Special Conference on Determinate Sentencing, University of California, 2–3 June 1977; published by the National Institute of Law Enforcement and Criminal Justice, March 1978).

24. Blumstein et al., *Research on Sentencing*, vol. 1, 211–12. See also Blumstein's essay, "The Impact of Changes in Sentencing Policy on Prison Populations," vol. 2, 460–89.

25. *Ibid.*, vol. 2, 484–85. Blumstein reports that a presentation to the Pennsylvania legislature of the population projections based on proposed new and heavier mandatory sentencing for several major crimes surprised a legislative committee into recommending a sentencing commission for detailed development and reviews of sentencing policy, a bill which was passed by one vote.

26. Cohen and Tonry, "Sentencing Reforms and Their Impacts," 353–411.

27. For a full account of the development of the Guidelines, see Don M. Gottfredson, Leslie T. Wilkins, and Peter B. Hoffman, *Guidelines for Parole and Sentencing* (Lexington, Mass.: Lexington Books, 1978). See also Blumstein et al., *Research on Sentencing*, vol. 1, 126–83, *passim*.

28. For a brief but cogent critique of the principle of descriptive guidelines, see the essay by Franklin M. Fisher and Joseph B. Kadane, "Empirically Based Sentencing Guidelines and Ethical Considerations," in Blumstein et al., *Research on Sentencing*, vol. 2, 184–93. In a complex consideration of the work of Gottfredson et al., Sparks raises but does not conclusively answer the question of the value of further refinement of the methodology employed, observing that if it is worthwhile to do further research then much more rigorous methods must be employed. See Richard F. Sparks, "The Construction of Sentencing Guidelines: A Methodological Critique," *ibid.*, 194–264.

29. A comprehensive but confusing account of the Minnesota experience with its Guide Lines Commission will be found in Susan E. Martin, "The Politics of Sentencing Reform: Sentencing Guidelines in Pennsylvania and Minnesota," *ibid.*, 265–304. Martin has attempted to compare the experience of the two states in creating a guidelines process by narrating the history of the two programs in parallel rather than in sequence. The Pennsylvania legislation was not nearly as successful as that in Minnesota for reasons that this author makes plain. It is clear that the Minnesota model will not necessarily succeed in every state that tries it, but Martin notes that Washington state has adopted it with some promise of success.

30. See Chaiken and Chaiken, *Varieties of Criminal Behavior*, 64ff.

31. United States Bureau of the Census, *Projections of the Population of the United States, by Age, Sex, and Race: 1983–2080* (Washington, D.C., May 1984). A projection so far into the next century is obviously subject to unpredictable contingencies. Note however that although a white male population of 13,748,000 in the 20 to 29 age group (4,611,000 less than in 1983) is predicted, the black population in the same age group will increase

during these same years from 2,757,000 to 3,370,000, an increase of 613,000. It is impractical to make a wager on the accuracy of these predictions, but the trend on which they are based has been fairly constant for many years.

32. John P. Conrad, "The Quandary of Dangerousness," *British Journal of Criminology* 22 (July 1982): 255–67. In this article I suggested that certain types of offender who might qualify as "dangerous" should be released from prison subject to the requirement of frequent (daily or weekly) reports to a bureau of police supervision, with further provision for field verification of the offender's activities. This plan was based on the perception that the police are better qualified and equipped to carry out surveillance than probation and parole officers. The objective of the plan was control through continuous information, to my mind a more reliable and less intrusive method than some of the electronic devices that have been proposed by high technology enthusiasts. Discussions of my proposal have had a mixed reception: Probation and parole officers generally hated the idea, but many police officers were receptive. So far the proposal has languished, and I am willing to accept the Georgia plan of Intensive Probation Supervision as a satisfactory and more generally acceptable alternative. For a brief account of Intensive Probation Supervision, see my article, "News of the Future: Research and Development in Corrections," *Federal Probation* 48(4) (December 1983): 54–55.

33. Personal communication from Billie S. Erwin, senior operations analyst, Georgia Department of Offender Rehabilitation, October 1984. Mrs. Erwin reports that a full report of her evaluation will be issued early in 1985.

Index

Abrahamse, Alan, 100–106
Age: of career criminal, 42, 43t, 59–60, 70–72, 71t; of juvenile offender, 32
Alcoholism, of career criminals, 60
American Bar Association, 23; model statutes drafted by, 123–24
American Law Institute, 22; model statutes drafted by, 123–24
Arrest rates, 79–80, 79t, 80t; of career criminals, 60, 62–63, 62t, 63t; of juvenile offenders, 35–37, 36t, 50, 51t; velocity of crimes and, 73–75
Autobiography of Benvenuto Cellini, 4

Base rate, of violent acts, 106
Baumes Act of 1926, 21
Beccaria, Cesare, 13, 25n.2, 91
Bentham, Jeremy: basic theorem of punishment of, 91; legacy of, 91–94, 108n.4. *See also* Utilitarianism
Benthamism: capital punishment in, 93, 109n.7; critique of, 92–93, 109n.6; decarceration argument of, 92, 109n.5; greater happiness principle of, 108n.3
Blacks: among juvenile offenders, 34; arrest rates of, 60; criminality of, 59; disproportionate number of crimes committed by, 137; sentencing discrimination against, 73; in underclass, 117
Blumstein, Alfred, 126

"Born criminal," 26n.7
Burton, Bob, 52

Calendar time, between arrests, 73
Capital: A Critique of Political Economy (Marx), 118
Capitalism, crime as consequence of, 119
Career criminal, 57–76; arrest frequencies of, 62–63; criminal histories of, 60–61, 61t, 72–75; criminal justice system and, 135–37; demographic characteristics of, 59–60, 70–72; dispositions of, 72–73; effect of prison experience on, 135–36; juvenile career of, 42–44, 43t; persistence of, 64–67; research design on, 58–59; retirement age of, 117; underclass and, 143n.8; specific deterence of, 80–83, 81t, 95–96; typology of, 105. *See also* Recidivism; Recidivists
Careers of the Violent (Miller, Dinitz, and Conrad), 2, 58, 74. *See also* Career criminal
Chaiken, Jan, 102, 105
Chaiken, Marcia, 102, 105
Challenge-and-response sequence, 1
Classification of offenders, 14
Clearance rates, 78–79, 79t, 83, 115, 142n.4; self-reporting of, 102
Cohen, Jacqueline, 103, 124, 126
Community supervision, of career criminals, 138–41, 147n.32; of juvenile offenders, 49
Conviction rates, 79, 79t, 80, 80t

About the Author

John P. Conrad was co-director of the Dangerous Offender Project, an undertaking of the Academy for Contemporary Problems, of Columbus, Ohio, where he was a senior fellow. He has served as a Senior Fulbright Fellow at the London School of Economics and as a visiting expert at the United Nations Asia and Far East Institute for the Prevention of Crime and the Treatment of Offenders at Fuchu, Japan. For 1982 to 1983 he was a visiting fellow at the National Institute of Justice in Washington, D.C.

Mr. Conrad received a bachelor's degree in political science at the University of California and a master's degree in social service administration at the University of Chicago. He has held teaching appointments at the University of California at Davis, the University of Pennsylvania, The Ohio State University, the Sam Houston State University, and the Simon Fraser University, where he is currently a visiting professor of criminology.

Most of his career has been spent in correctional services. For twenty years he worked in various capacities in the California Department of Corrections. In 1967 he was appointed chief of research of the United States Bureau of Prisons. He later served as chief of the Center for Crime Prevention and Rehabilitation of the National Institute of Law Enforcement and Criminal Justice, now the National Institute of Justice. From 1974 to 1976 he was chief editor of the *Journal of Research in Crime and Delinquency*. Since 1977 he has conducted in *Federal Probation* a column on criminological research and development, entitled "News of the Future."

He is the author of *Justice and Consequences* (Lexington Books, 1981) and co-author, with Ernest van den Haag, of *The Death Penalty: A Debate* (Plenum, 1983).